Principals with Impact aligns the demanding routine of a 21st century school principal with the best of theoretical knowledge and practical frameworks to ensure successful leadership. Filled with stories and examples from his years of experience, Dr. Jaeger presents five distinct roles to better understand how effective principals can meet the challenges of leading and enhancing the teaching and learning process. School administrators and professors will gain much from reading this well-written book, most likely to soon be on every principal's bookshelf.

Jan Hammond, Ed.D.
Professor Emerita, State University of New York at New Paltz

Principals With Impact is an excellent resource for principals who are committed to transforming our educational systems. The book presents five critical roles effective school leaders assume to provide an extraordinary learning environment for teachers and students. Dr. Jaeger uses case studies and sound principles to empower bold thinking and actions that prompt school leaders to take on new ways for training teachers and improving students' learning outcomes.

Valerie J. Lyons, MSED, LMHC
Assistant Director of Student Affairs, Hunter College, City University of New York
Graduate Program Advisor for School Counselors - School of Education

At the heart of all Dr. Jaeger's work is his honest enthusiasm for developing collective responsibility to provide students, teachers, and school leaders with the support necessary to be successful. You will be left with a clear vision for educational excellence and an action plan for success. He is a visionary, true instructional leader, and will be an asset to any educational organization.

Dr. Linda Heitmann
Past Deputy Superintendent, Dutchess County BOCES (NY)

What makes Dr. Jaeger unique is his expert combination of deep professional knowledge, coaching skill and collegial expertise. He enables, focuses and collaborates with others around essential purposes, instructional effectiveness and future possibilities among school staff and schools.

Mae Fong
Former School Principal and CEI Site-Based School Specialist – New York City Schools

I look forward to Lloyd's training. He breaks down the material with clarity and application. With active listening, he engages and responds to individual and group needs as training occurs.

Michael Tierney
Superintendent of Schools, Dover Union Free School District

Dr. Jaeger is a master educator, an expert on-site coach for school principals, an on-line workshop designer and facilitator within a new teacher induction system, and an invaluable program development colleague.

Frank San Felice
Past Project Director, The Center for Educational Innovation (CEI), New York City

Dr. Jaeger is a consultant with the rare ability to enhance and provide exceptional and caring leadership that builds education communities. His thoughtful, experienced and cogent analysis of issues at hand never fails to bring insight and creative practical contributions to any project and project team. He is so often the one who summarizes the critical elements of what needs to be done and provides a way forward.

Maria L DeWald
Former Member: New York State Professional Standards and Practices Board for Teaching
Past President - NYS Parent Teacher Association

Dr. Jaeger is a strategic thinker, who possesses a mastery of language and helps organizations and staffs take an honest look at themselves.

Dr. Paul Finch
Past Superintendent of Schools, Red Hook (NY) Central School District

PRINCIPALS
with
IMPACT

5

LEADERSHIP ROLES TO IMPROVE SCHOOLS

DR. LLOYD JAEGER
BEST SELLING AUTHOR

ISBN: 978-1-949513-17-2

Publisher The DP Group, LLC

Acknowledgments and Dedication

If you have enjoyed a public television program, then you know well the deeply toned PBS announcer's statement, "This program has been made possible through the generous donations of the XYZ Foundation and contributions from viewers like you." Similarly, if no man is an island, then my life, my career and by extension this book have been made possible through the generous contributions of countless mentors, colleagues, developers, and advocates. I dedicate this book to paying forward all you have given me.

Mom and Dad – As parents, you modeled excellence and created boundless opportunities to develop friends and be one in the world. You valued service and lived it daily as active church leaders and community volunteers within every school and school district I ever attended.

Woody – Amherst might never have stretched me to learn how to learn, to think and to communicate with a confident voice if you had not brought me to meet Dean Wilson.

Reverend Koenig and Dr. Rounds – You solidified my direction. Giving the gift of the spirit was not limited to the Sabbath day, it could be given to students every day. And so, I chose teaching.

Walker, Meaney, Lyon, Russo, Foy, Hains, Roswencz, Levin, Anderson, Smith and Mann – My teachers one and all. That I became an educator who expected rigor and strove to achieve ambitious goals with students and colleagues are your legacies.

Pat, Frank, Linda, Connie, Eileen, Debbie, Jeff and Brett – Many principals I've known were good, but you were my constellation of stars. You touched teachers and you changed your schools.

Vivian – You always said there was a book inside me. I've done it my sister!

Erica – My dear and accomplished daughter … Your advice ultimately unlocked my morass. "Don't try to boil the ocean, Dad. Just pick an entry point and tell your story from there."

Divya – Authoring is demanding work. It is a mountain to climb, at least it has been for me. Your coaching focused me and lit my path. I couldn't have done this without you.

Brian and Frank – Lifelong colleagues, I trusted you to give me early and unvarnished feedback. It was scary to surrender my drafts, but your eyes were receptive, and your comments moved me forward.

Beth Ann – Two years in the making, you have been behind me always, enduring long hours of me squirreled away with a laptop. I'm not sure anyone but you could have given me this gift, space and unconditional encouragement.

Thank you all!

TABLE OF CONTENTS

My Heartfelt Message for You

Let Our Conversation Begin

This book is my gift to you. Its concepts and principles, its utilities and resources, and its purposes and aspirations are golden threads I have teased out from the woven tapestry of my long and continuing career. These pay homage to the highly effective principals I have known. You have transformed schools time and time again. Your influences have been far-reaching, and the lessons I have derived from our partnering together have inspired me to write *Principals with Impact*.

Page by page, chapter by chapter, role by role, and recommendation by recommendation, let us sit comfortably as two committed colleagues in an extended conversation about this profession we hold dear. Let's explore how extraordinary principals leverage and share their leadership. Let's come to understand how these leaders engage their school in shifting its present trajectories toward yet to be accomplished possibilities.

As we begin, I realize that as my committed colleague, you may be one of many possible persons. Clearly, you could be a practicing principal, although potentially, you are an aspiring one. Perhaps you lead, coach, or supervise principals. Alternatively, you may teach within a higher education matriculation program, providing pathways to earn school administrator certification. You might have a more itinerant role as a contract consultant who develops school leaders, introducing them to meaningful skills that augment their professional repertoire. Finally, you might be a researcher or journalist, seeking to capture educational trends to assimilate them into the broader literature and discussion of our field. Whatever your role, you cannot underestimate the importance of your influence on our future educational system. Whatever you have accomplished for educators, schools, or communities to date, may this book extend your reach, increase your impact, and provide means and methods you might not have considered in quite the combination offered here.

Our conversation's context is within the broad contours and incredible variance of America's education system. Across fifty separate states, it is at once robust and enabling, while in reality, its door-opening opportunities function less consistently or inclusively. Color, ethnicity, gender, religion, and earnings continue to make a difference. Zip codes matter. Like a diamond, our system may be seen for its gleaming and polished facets, although its inner fault lines may reveal flaws that portend its ongoing fragility. While our universities remain magnets for global learners, our PK-12 schools no longer shine as the world's beacon of student results.

It is staggering that these trends would be so considering our recent history. Both the Federal Title I legislation with all its billions flowing to educate the disadvantaged and the Title IX law that has promoted and served to regulate gender equities now straddle either side of a 50-year marker since enacted. The weighty proclamations and proposed remedies published in *A Nation at Risk*[1] with great fanfare are now nearly four decades old. During successive administrations, major initiatives followed, such as the national curriculum standards movement, *Goals 2000*, the *No Child Left Behind* and *Every Child Succeeds* Acts, and finally, the latest reauthorization of *the Elementary and Secondary Schools Act (ESSA)*. Each turned on the federal faucet, streaming cash into state and local coffers in the name of school improvement. They served as a continuum of national "reforms de jour." Over time, they have neither healed American education's flaws and fragility, nor have they thoroughly disrupted its overall inertia. Even now, our facts are stubborn. Across this land every day, schools live with excellence and inequity as well as competence and dysfunction.

Between the covers of this volume, you'll note that I have chosen to focus on the individual school as the unit for systemic change. However, in my experience, typically, normative teaching cultures tend not to self-generate or promote universal principles of practice that will contribute to students' growth, development, and learning. By contrast and without question, my best schools have always had extremely talented principals who engender remarkable staff focus and collaboration. These schools have been able to achieve the highest and most positive student outcomes. I wish this for each of you. While not a recipe book per se, *Principals with Impact* provides my witness to how principals have led with influence and impact to elevate both teacher and student performance.

Let me close this initial conversation with all my respect and acknowledgment. As a Principal, you have chosen to do something extraordinary. You must be indefatigable and frequently courageous. Your daily work is expansive, demanding, and perhaps all too often a lonely struggle to serve others.

You are accountable and responsible for the safety of youth. You support and supervise professionals. Your community needs clear communication. In short, life for you is not a game show. There are no prizes awarded for the right answers, and there is rarely a "phone a friend" option to address your latest confounding challenge or to brainstorm how to respond to the derailment of the day. The fact is that forward progress is not a straight-lined pathway, even with the clearest of goals and the best-laid plans. To achieve

---

1   United States. National Commission on Excellence in Education. A Nation at Risk: The Imperative for Educational Reform: A Report to the Nation and the Secretary of Education, United States Department of Education. Washington, D.C.: The Commission: [Supt. of Docs., U.S. G.P.O. distributor], 1983.

much, you might have to overcome more. After all, schools are human organizations frequently fraught with unexpected issues.

Nevertheless, with an optimistic and constructive stance, I assert that no matter where you are or what you're up against, you can turn the page of your current history and write the next chapter of your school's future. With your experience and wisdom, virtually any daily issue can be grounds for a fresh beginning. It can be the premise for drawing a new line in your sand by declaring, "*This must change. As we work and strive together, we shall achieve new outcomes.*" I wish you Godspeed, and in the pages ahead, let us take this journey together.

Introduction

Every school principal shares a critical imperative and is beholden to an implicit promise. You are responsible for causing the growth and development of those who teach and those who learn. Fundamental to your leadership is your obligation to elevate the performance of your students and your faculty. As for student's families, you commit that you are bonded to the implied promise of all schools; that their children will have more than a random chance to succeed at your school. Theirs will not be default futures, but instead will become possible futures. Your imperative, therefore, is of clear and unrelenting purpose. To the best of your abilities, you will prepare and enable your staff to provide each of your school's children with sustained opportunities to grow, develop, succeed, and achieve.

With these understandings in mind, I begin this volume unequivocally. Schools are results-oriented organizations, and your school's outcomes do matter. Collectively, you and your staff will embrace bold visions that never before were deemed worthy of pursuing, possible to accomplish, or reasonable to achieve. You will engender and give rise to a school community that values working together. Together you will plan with focused purpose and undertake intentional actions to progress in their realization. In the end and during the period of your leadership, you will have created and left a legacy. Simply put, the students and teachers of your schools will have the will and the sustainable means to elevate their performance. And by design, you will have spawned a trajectory of elevated school results.

Principals with Impact is a compendium of useful concepts, principles, resources, and illustrations to guide your efforts. Based on my thousands of direct interactions with principals, it "cuts to the chase" with specific integrative supports and tools you may use to establish a shared vision, to collaborate effectively, to improve professional expertise, and to exceed your goals. It will not be an easy undertaking, but in deference to the promises that we must keep, each principal must enjoin staff to take the shared journey to bold futures for all students. You need the means to do so.

Over the years, I have discerned five critical roles effective principals assume and then perform to elevate school performance. These have proven applicable in rural and urban settings, in small and large schools of any grade span, and in profoundly diverse or strongly homogeneous communities. These effective principals have improved school results. Within a school's culture, they helped to develop shared agreements and shared outcomes providing the impetus to guide teaching and learning. These schools monitored progress toward common goals one student, and one staff member at a time. The five roles effective principals employed to elevate school performance are:

- The Preacher
- The Surveyor
- The Developer
- The Collaborator
- The Craftsman

Each role is unique and will contribute essential aspects to your overall process of increasing staff efficacy and engaging students in rigorous learning. Each chapter illuminates a single role's core purposes and functions. As the chapters progress, the roles are increasingly cross-referenced and integrated to represent the reality that a principal's work is multidimensional. It is also characterized by simultaneity. The fact is that principals must attend daily to routine responsibilities, new regulations or requirements, and phased implementation of new initiatives. Thus, no principal acts singularly in one role at a time. To this crucial point, the chapters will demonstrate how each role can influence and support the other as you accomplish your important goals.

I invite you to peruse the book and read it in accordance with your needs. Though presented sequentially, scanning all five chapter summaries could be an excellent way to familiarize yourself with all the roles before doing a deep dive into any one of them. I would rather you think of the book as a basis for conversation with me at your side. Where do you want to begin our conversation, given what you've skimmed or read? What jumps out as relevant or applicable? Why that chapter or role? What are you facing? How may I support you? Every possibility is an excellent starting point for our chat, precisely because you are the expert. Only you know where you are and what you are trying to accomplish. You also know your staff's strengths and their relative needs for development.

The pages are yours to turn. The conversations are ours to have. As you apply them to your school's needs and opportunities, please do so through the lens of every principal's imperative. Elevate your school's performance. Enable your staff to launch new approaches and generate new student learning trajectories toward goals you have yet to achieve. Though you have already chosen to do this extraordinary work, be undeterred in realizing these ambitions. For this and so much more, I acknowledge you! I trust this book honors the significant importance of being a school leader!

Dr. Lloyd Jaeger
Orlando, Florida - 2020

CHAPTER ONE

ROLE ONE

THE PREACHER

From the time of the Greeks, preachers have used the artful power of oratory with audiences across cultures, time, and place. Their communication serves to inform, to inspire, to convey, to enlighten, to encourage, to influence, and to persuade. Though frequently associated with the secular practice, preachers' messages need not be. In fact, preachers do also address non-secular gatherings in distinctively public settings. More importantly, preaching is grounded in a point of view, a moral or professional code, a set of values, an ethical stance, a way of understanding the world both as it is, and as a prospective rationale for how it might be. Preachers seek to induce a variety of responses, among others, including reflection, understanding, growth, alignment, commitment, connection, and action.

For principals, assuming the role of a preacher is a potent influence among your staff. Your speech, what you say, and why you say it gives purpose and direction. It articulates why, how, and to what ends you will do your work together. It enables you to distinguish this work from many other professions. Education is not, for example, a job that punches a clock dispassionately or provides five-star hospitality services. We don't manufacture widgets, nor do we operate resort hotels with arrays of pampering luxury services targeted for the rich and famous.

What we do is grow and enable the next generation of youth to join us in leading, serving, and being citizens of the world. We have the opportunity to heal hearts and minds. We get to model and be a stand for contributing to what is right and distinguishing it from what is wrong. We act to protect the least among us. We provide the tools for building and creating. We open minds, bodies, and spirits to the arts, and with it, we encourage self-expression. Our students learn and use knowledge to understand, to discern, and to problem-solve. They practice and apply skills to read, to communicate, to do, to resolve, to investigate, and to compete. We can go on. In short, educators are professionals charged with opening doors to students' future and inspiring every child with the acquired capacities for pursuing a life of possibility.

When you assume the Preacher role, you get to call your staff to action for impassioned and meaningful purposes; that is, human purposes that are bigger than ourselves.

Mobilizing is Job One for Principals

Job one for school principals is to mobilize your school and community with a visioning process that will move others to action. These intentional interactions will culminate in you having a commonly understood and accepted core purpose. For me, it has always been that students deserve to grow into a bold and ambitiously identified future, not a probable and satisfactory future. To mobilize, then, is to involve your school staff, students, parents, and community members in deliberative conversations that will result in collective and coordinated actions to fulfill your shared purpose and vision.

While in theory mobilizing can commence at any time, mobilizing as Job 1 connotes urgency. There are no laurels to rest on as a school principal.

Whatever your school's current state, or however recently you have become its leader; your imperative is to elevate performance. In my view, the ultimate goal is to grow and to remain a consistently improving school. Working to these ends, you must routinely scan school practices and analyze operative principles to identify the next areas for refinement, enhancement, evolution, revision, inclusion, adaptation, and reinvention. What is at stake is nothing less than the scope and possibilities for your students' futures.

Essential Questions for Mobilizing

About our Responsibilities

Are we doing what we should be?

Are we where we should be?

Are we headed in the direction we need to be?

About our Possibilities

Where do we want to go?

Are there new options we want to undertake?

What new accomplishments do we wish to achieve?

About our Results

Are we moving toward our goal(s)?

Are we accomplishing what we committed to?

What indicators tell us that this is so?

Please be assured that I don't wish to overlook or treat as insignificant the array of forward-leaning actions your school-community might be taking. With that acknowledged, though, mobilizing or re-mobilizing with relevant others can occur at any time. Principals do this by consistently posing several essential questions (see sidebar).

Translated differently, principals consistently inquire if they (and their school) are on the right path, going in the right direction, and what evidence helps themselves and others to decide if they are. Assuming the role of the Preacher is an invaluable first step.

Coined originally by President Theodore Roosevelt, the term "bully pulpit" has commonly referred to the speeches and writings of persons who have positions of public prominence. Using their public roles to influence, they espouse and advocate for a particular point of view. They describe their assessment of what the current reality is and is not. Preachers may also offer a future vision of what is possible to achieve. Utilizing a "bully pulpit" approach offers exciting opportunities to coalesce support from some and collective action among others. Leaders must motivate and mobilize followers, for without followers, there can be no sustainable actions and results. "Bully pulpits" can help leaders to gain the necessary attention to attract the followers who will commit to a future of shared meaning.

As a school principal, you are a person who holds such a prominent position. You have access to your own "bully pulpit." From the start, therefore, it is worth considering what will motivate and influence your school community to follow or collaborate with you. How will you employ the powers of your bully pulpit to mobilize others? We begin by illustrating one dominant approach.

Rhonda Vasquez was the new Assistant Superintendent for Instruction (ASI) of a small urban school system. One week on the job, she was called to the superintendent's office and handed the State Education Department's Annual School and District Report Card detailing student performance results on the previous year's state examinations. The superintendent informed Rhonda that in her new role as ASI, she would present this report to the Board of Education (BOE) two weeks later, along with a plan to respond effectively to the results. Of the four elementary schools, three had average school-wide reading and writing scores below state proficiency standards. Among these three, the magnet elementary school served the district's highest concentration of non-white economically disadvantaged youth, and it had among the lowest set of language arts test scores in its county of 13 school systems. Only 53% of the magnet school's students had achieved proficient state performance levels.

As the new kid on the block, Rhonda Vasquez had no "cred" (credibility) with the principal team or the district's faculty. Frankly, for them, it did not matter that her incoming resume package contained well-documented positive results and highly endorsed professional references taken from her many previous school and district system assignments. What mattered, though, for Rhonda Vasquez was that the facts were clear on three fronts. First, the principals had been doing whatever they had been doing to enable precisely the results their respective schools had gotten. Additionally, the faculty had been teaching and assessing students in ways that had enabled exactly the results their students had received. Finally, the state's results were at hand, and they were seriously subpar. Exacerbating circumstances was the fact that the local newspapers had just published the test scores of all the region's fifty-two elementary schools and shined a particular spotlight on her new district's poor results.

It was in this context that she was directed by her new superintendent to make a public report to the Board of Education. It was to be about the latest state test scores, and it was on the schedule for its next meeting in less than two weeks. The potential ahead was ominous. One scenario Rhonda could play out was to declare the metaphorical and biblical equivalent of how it had been torrentially raining low-performance indicators among the district's children. Everyone knew a predictable flood of lousy test scores would be coming, but no one had built an ark to save the students. Rhonda Vasquez's first public report might very well have become a comprehensive "blame game," with both the principals and the faculty awash in the subsequent fallout.

What occurred was something entirely different. Rhonda declared to the BOE that, based on the state's results, "improving student literacy was going to be our most important job for the foreseeable future!" The district would engage the staff in examining its curricula, acquiring and aligning appropriate curricular materials, and participating in system-wide professional development. This effort would translate into student comprehension and written expression scores that would improve annually. No one was blamed. Rhonda Vasquez asked principals to lead a vision of a possible future, i.e., that every school would meet or exceed state proficiency standards and that at least 85-90% of all students would meet or exceed state reading and written proficiency levels within three years.

What happened? All schools accomplished these goals with more than 85% of all students exceeding state language arts standards. In addition, one of the four elementary schools achieved the county's highest student proficiency rate within only two years.

Rhonda Vasquez's story points to how one may use a "bully pulpit" to coalesce action without relying upon declarative, blame-oriented commentary. Rallying others toward new futures can leave the past in the past. On the other hand, there is a startling reality we should examine. For over a decade, student performance results in each elementary school had patterned well below state standards. Excuses ran rampant as cover for subpar student performance. It was common to hear, "What can we expect from students in a community like ours?" However, this universal cry also exposed an undiscussed and unchallenged truth. Any one of the principals could have brought forth critically needed shifts at their school at any time. Rhonda's central office bully pulpit, though laudably used, didn't need to be the impetus for improving literacy in that central school system. What she did understand was that purpose-filled visions could catalyze, drive, and clarify the actions necessary to achieve the results embodied in that vision. Rhonda had employed the strategic elements for elevating school performance: Vision – Purpose – Action – Results.

The Rhonda Vasquez lesson for principals is that past performance need not and should not predetermine future results. Mobilizing others at the individual school level must be Job One. Said differently, it is and will always be the students (and their families) who take the journey of your school's educational experiences. It is their destination, their opportunities, and their results that you must articulate in the school's vision. The vision will be aspirational, motivational, and dispose the school's constituencies to create and take action. When assessed, the results will provide evidence for realizing and extending the vision in perpetual questing for a more positive future.

Using your "bully pulpit" creates essential preconditions for mobilizing and moving with others toward a new future. For it begins to provide answers for essential questions:

Why must we change now?

How might we do so?

How might we evolve?

Why is that reasonable and important for us to do?

Moonshot Thinking

What does "mobilizing" look and sound like in language? How do words resonate from a bully pulpit to engage and then call others to action? While aspirational and motivational style serves to articulate a vision, it will be questions that guide the collective efforts, inquiry, development, decision-making, problem defining, and problem-solving of others. These are the persons who will mobilize to become your partners and collaborators in action.

President John F. Kennedy at Rice University. NASA, PD.

President John F. Kennedy's 1962 Moon Speech is a virtual template of such bully pulpit language. It has both the elements of a future vision and the questions that would mobilize others to action. Notably, his use of powerful oratory sought to move America beyond any of its perceived current limits to a future world that had yet to be conceived or achieved. I refer to this as calling a moonshot:

"Why go to the moon? **We choose to go** *to the moon [i.e., fly a man safely there and return him to earth]* **in this decade** *and do the other things,* **not because they are easy, but because they are hard,** *because* **that goal will serve to organize and measure the best of our energies and skills,** *because* **that challenge is one that we are willing to accept, one we are unwilling to postpone, and one which we intend to win,** *and the others, too."*

Inspired by the Kennedy Speech, what is your equivalent of a "moonshot?" That is to say:

Moonshot Essential Questions

What is the goal that will serve to organize and measure the best of your school's energy and skills?

What is the challenge you are willing to accept and to postpone no longer?

What is the challenge you intend to win?

What things will you do, not because they are easy but because they are hard?

By when will you get to where you intend to go? In what period of time?

Most importantly, have you expressed and called your moonshot in publicly shared language?

The power of moonshot thinking is in you making the case that exceeding what is presently real or even possible is necessary and worthy as part of an inspired and shared future.

With a moonshot now called, what will "mobilizing" language begin to look and sound like? I suggest using the notions of "Current State – Desired Future" as part of the yin and yang for your moonshot thinking and language. You'll quickly note this correlation within the Kennedy speech. You begin by developing answers to a broad initial question (see sidebar).

A school-based example of moonshot thinking is the case of Kasey Samuels, Principal of a 7-12 Junior-Senior High School. She knew the current research on reading and comprehension --- that using Independent, Instructional, and Frustration level text materials have a different impact on student learning. To her, middle and secondary schools (hers included) often mistakenly served up textbooks and other text-based classroom materials with little regard for text difficulty. As a consequence, learning in her

Desired State Essential Questions

What needs to happen to move your school from your "Current State" of practice and results to your "Desired Future?

That question leads to a series of other issues to clarify and focus on:

What is your school's Current State or Status?

What is working and what is not working?

What future external or internal factors may influence how your current state or desired future will evolve or change?

Based on what descriptors or body of evidence?

In your considerations, for who does your Current State analysis and Desired Future apply?

Students?

Families?

Community?

Staff?

All of the above?

By when will you and others achieve your Desired Future?

school and student achievement results suffered. She resolved to change these patterns.

For Kasey, teachers calibrating their use of texts in the classroom and for reading homework was a bit analogous to understanding the children's story when Goldilocks discovered the Three Bears had left their separate porridge bowls on the table when they went out for a walk. Upon sampling each, Goldilocks found the first was served too hot; that is, teachers required students to use text materials well beyond their comprehension. Research referred to such texts as being at students' frustration levels with a predictive comprehension level of less than 50%, even with teacher instruction related to the books. When Goldilocks tasted the second porridge bowl it was served too cold; that is, textbooks or other text prompts were way too easy. The students could already read it independently without any mediating teacher instruction. Then, and often in actuality, students were not stretched in any way to understand the content or prose because they could already comprehend 90% or more of these texts' meanings. Over the long run, Kasey knew that engaging students routinely with either under or overchallenging texts presented risk. Student growth and understanding were often compromised and not spawned.

Finally, there was the last bear's porridge bowl. Goldilocks felt it was just the right temperature. As such, it was highly edible, and she consumed the bowlful. Kasey knew that this correlated with teachers providing and mediating texts that were at an instructional level. These texts were both challenging and growth oriented. They were not too far above students' heads and were not sent home as independent reading homework without prior instruction. With the right in-class teacher support (i.e., scaffolding), students could stretch their understanding and comprehension to not less than 75% of these texts' meanings, even in the face of their challenge.

The moonshot Kasey ultimately called was to prepare all students for 9th grade high school entrance with sufficient reading readiness to comprehend all high school level texts independently. Impossible as that seemed, why did she press for that goal? She had observed that too often high school texts were overmatched for many high school readers. They were written at students' frustration level (50%

comprehension). Kasey reasoned that if teachers requiring students to complete independent level reading was going to continue as part of routine homework, then student capacities for reading had to be at or above high school level text difficulty. The increased capacity would enable students to comprehend 90% or more of assigned reading homework independently and provide the basis for greater understanding when returning for classroom discourse and activities the next day.

In the alternative, more challenging texts had to be mediated in class with teacher support before being assigned as homework. In this way, students would meet their instructional levels, and at least 75% or more comprehension could occur when the students completed their homework reading. All of this was especially important as the school began to push for more classroom inquiry, investigation, debate, and discussion at a higher order of thinking levels.

Kasey's called moonshot was a collective call to develop student reading comprehension in all junior high content areas and to create cohorts of high school commencement level readers as a 9th-grade local entry-level standard. At the time she began this quest, less than 33% of 9th graders had 12th-grade independent comprehension levels. The journey to shift that was not going to be easy. It was going to be hard. In the Kennedy tradition, it was a challenge she was unwilling to postpone any longer. It was a moonshot. The postscript? Three years later, reading achievement had risen for entering 9th graders such that 75% could read a college-level text independently with 90% comprehension.

The genius of moonshot thinking is not only that it projects and states an ambitious and desired future, but that it contains a requirement that mobilizing action must follow. To recall, President Kennedy described this when he declared, "that goal [landing a man on the moon and returning him safely to earth] will serve to organize and measure the best of our energies and skills." He did not suggest we knew how to go to the moon, but he did declare that "we" would organize, collaborate, and apply our energy and skills to get there.

In earlier discussion examples, school leaders Rhonda Vasquez and Kasey Samuels both declared moonshots involving student literacy. For each, there was an embedded and implicit commitment to engage staff in future professional learning so that they could enable students to develop advanced student literacy competencies. We shall refer to this as having a Theory of Action.

As modeled below, a Theory of Action begins with an overarching essential question, which is supported and developed further with a set of related questions. It initiates a period of collective inquiry through which you and your staff can identify essential principles and practices that are characteristic of "Current State" teaching and learning, as well as forecast what must be sought after and learned as a precondition for realizing your schools "Desired Future."

Theory of Action Essential Questions

What is our Theory of Action to achieve or accomplish our desired future?

What are the set of professional research, sources, and in-service training regarding high leverage and impactful teaching, learning, and assessment about which we already know?

To which of these best practices are we committed? Which are we using?

Of those in use and those yet to be utilized, which will we select as the essential pedagogic concepts and principles for engaging students as they progress toward accomplishing our vision and purpose for them?

What research-based best practices do we believe we still have to learn to achieve our vision for students?

Following the inquiry period, The Theory of Action process concludes with a publicly stated hypothesis, as depicted in the diagram and language on the next page.

A Theory of Action

From This

WHAT IS OUR SCHOOL'S THEORY OF ACTION FOR IMPROVING STUDENT RESULTS?

To This

CURRENT STATE

WHAT NEEDS TO HAPPEN?

DESIRED FUTURE

If _____,
(If we commit to doing "x")

then _____
will happen,

resulting in _____.
(Desired Future described with specificity, metrics or deliverables)

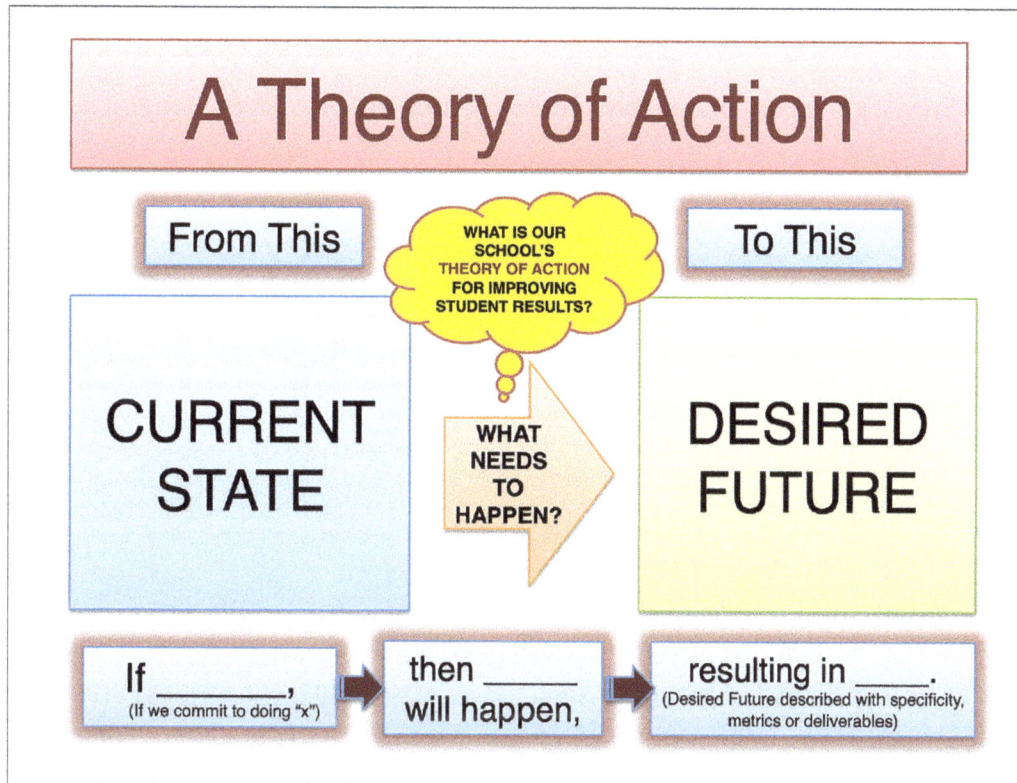

If we commit to doing _____ with consistency and fidelity, then we expect _____ to happen (for or with _____), resulting in _____ (the desired future as evidenced by _____).

Implicit in all this language modeling is a fundamental premise; that **as a principal, you assume responsibility for developing and utilizing a shared language within the public and professional domains of your school**. In inquiring about it and inventing that language, you and your staff will empower each other to engage in the necessary work of growing and improving your capacities to serve your students, parents, and communities.

Extending the Vasquez and Samuels Stories

When Rhonda Vasquez and Kasey Samuels publicly committed to improving student literacy, they set both the foundational vision and purpose for the Theory of Action hypothesis and subsequent collective actions their school staff would undertake. A synthesized version of their Theory of Action is modeled below. Please take note of the three-part language structure used when articulating a Theory of Action hypothesis: If _____, then _____ will happen, resulting in _____ (with desired future outcomes or metrics).

Illustrating the Vasquez and Samuels Theory of Action

If all our staff are provided with appropriate:

Training,

Modeling, and

Coaching,

So that they employ research-based pedagogic practices for developing:

Student reading comprehension and

Written expression skills,

Then our students will:

Demonstrate increasingly higher individual proficiency levels,

Meet or exceed state language arts benchmark measures, and

Be prepared to undertake rigorous college-bound inquiry and learning within their high school coursework.

Clearly, I am asserting that as a principal, you have the bully pulpit opportunity to introduce and articulate a commitment to a moonshot, born in inquiry questions, and shared in Theory of Action language to accomplish the desired future. Furthermore, you need not and must not be constrained or beholden to your current state (including the beliefs and capacities about what others deem to be currently possible). Moonshot Thinking will be your Vision and Purpose. A Theory of Action hypothesis will articulate your pathway to Action and Results. In any event, it is your principal's imperative to have and employ a strategic process for elevating your school's performance. For me, that process has always included a combination of clarifying and identifying what is true of my current state, and then collaborating with staff to focus and commit in mobilized action toward a desired future. In short, **Principals with Impact regularly originate and employ these four elements: Vision – Purpose – Action – Results.**

The Preacher
Endnotes

The Principal as Preacher

- Uses one's "bully pulpit" to induce others' reflection, inquiry, understanding, growth, alignment, commitment, and connection.
- Expresses "Moonshot Thinking" that challenges others to move beyond perceived current limits and toward a future world that has yet to be conceived or achieved.
- Mobilizes his or her school and community with a visioning process that engages and motivates relevant others to take action toward that vision.
- Initiates staff and/or community inquiry to clarify one's current state, including its principles and practices, as well as what must be sought after and learned as preconditions for realizing one's desired future.
- States a publicly expressed Theory of Action that articulates a hypothesis of the actions and processes that will lead one's school from its current state toward its desired future.

In summary, the Preacher's language is a principal's tool for engaging one's school community in the inquiries and communication necessary to elevate school performance. The principal's Preacher-oriented language and the community's subsequent shared language will give rise to the strategic four-element process identified as Vision - Purpose - Action – Results. As Preacher, the principal will:

- Engage in Moonshot Thinking to express Vision and Purpose.
- Clarify and identify the characteristics of your school's Current State.
- Envision and describe the Desired Future in terms of aspirational results or alternative outcomes distinguished from the Current State.
- Formulate a hypothesis expressed as a Theory of Action defining the actions that, if taken, will accomplish those results and outcomes.
- Focus staff commitment and mobilize staff action toward the Desired Future.

CHAPTER TWO

ROLE TWO

THE SURVEYOR

Surveyors use a complex combination of tools, geographic measurements, analytic skills, and knowledge of materials to study, record, and inform engineering and construction considerations. For example, their data and assessments are crucial for the design and development of a navigable road between two locations. You need only visualize a mountain in between them to grasp how a surveyor's work will enlighten any determination to go over rather than around it. In schools, principals often need to accomplish the equivalent.

When assuming the Surveyor role, principals begin with an inquiry: "What do I need to understand to bring my school from its current point A to a future and desired point of B?" Like surveyors, principals must ascertain and reveal the facts on their school's metaphorical ground and then map out the terrain ahead. Fundamentally, principals must assess their circumstances and plot out pathways for moving their school-community from its current state toward a desired future. To accomplish this, principals adapt and transpose a whole series of surveyor-like questions. These include:

What's the "lay of the land" around here?

What's it like at our intended destination?

Can the land (or conditions) ahead support the new home (school) we want to build (or create)?

What will be required to construct an adequate, safe, and passable road (of program and/or professional development) on which to journey to our new destination?

How will I prepare my staff to make and then take this journey?

Supposing there is a proverbial mountain in front of us ...

    Can we evolve current practice(s) to go around it?

    Or must we tunnel through it with new tools and excavations?

If instead we have the equivalent of a dense and unavoidable forest ahead, what are our development choices and at what cost?

    Do we cut down the whole forest (to transform everything)?

    Or do we preserve treasured portions of the forest?

    Or do we systematically cut a direct swath through it?

Who owns our land (the current patterns and practices of our school)?

Who asserts authority over its operation (boards, government, labor)?

Do particular laws, historical status, or significant designations protect the land (perhaps state regulations for tested outcomes)?

Do I/We need to negotiate the equivalent of a right of way among persons with vested interests in "the ways things work" around here (perhaps a new labor contract)?

Does the property (current conditions) need to be condemned (challenged) and otherwise seized (stopped) as a declaration of eminent domain for an essential public interest (like protecting the welfare of students or ensuring appropriate equities among personnel)?

Let me be clear. When principals act as surveyors, you are assuming an absolute and necessary responsibility. **You must understand clearly and at the most rigorous level how your staff are performing as teachers, how well they are influencing learning, and finally, the extent to which students are improving and achieving as learners. Only then can you consider their readiness for the actions you will or must take to accomplish the ambitious goals of the Preacher's moonshot thinking.** Chapters Three and Four will go on to explain the means for you to develop your staff and collaborate with them to design and construct the road to your new destination. In this chapter, however, act as a surveyor. Explore how you can be systematic in learning where you actually are and what is ahead of you. Then, with this information, you will be introduced to practices to identify your options, carve out the right pathways and take the journey forward.

No Corks on Your Watch

L et's begin with an illuminating story about both accountability and responsibility.

It was a cold wintry afternoon. The snow-filled wind whistled briskly in sweeping drifts across the surrounding property and fields. Though the school was closed, and the silent hallways no longer echoed with the vitality of children, the library was alive with intensely pivotal interchanges that might well shape the futures of those assembled.

Around a room-sized horseshoe of rearranged tables, all the district's school principals and assistant principals gathered as crucial stakeholders in the retiring superintendent's search and replacement process. Jack Lowden, the superintendent candidate, sat centered and facing the group. Late in the ensuing interview, the assembled administrators invited Jack to share any concluding thoughts or questions he might have.

Exhilarated, as he felt things had gone well thus far, Jack also felt anxious for this offered a defining moment to plant the seeds of his philosophy that would either get him the job with his future leadership team or not. Having anticipated there might be this opening, Jack reached into his suit jacket pocket to retrieve and give each administrator a small bottle stopper cork. "There are three kinds of schools," he said. "Improving Schools, Declining Schools, and Corks. With you, I want to be a part of creating improving schools in which students and their families have a better educational experience than had been available to them before we got here. They deserve to have that promise fulfilled.

Then there are declining schools. Simply put, I believe we are obliged to intervene when there are warning signs and turn them around if the indicators are already there. We must keep the hopes and promise of schooling alive and available for every student and family.

Finally, and most importantly, let's be sure that during our time together, there are no corks among our schools; that is those schools that just drift aimlessly like corks on the ocean's surface - they are going nowhere. For that matter, when we think about our teachers and school staff who serve our students and families, let's engender a climate that expects and enables them to improve continually. Let's observe and intervene appropriately when their performance is adrift like a cork or even struggling and in decline.

At the end of the day, I believe this leadership team has both the opportunity and the responsibility to pursue improvement persistently. To accomplish this, we must establish a shared vision and direction for where we are going, and then cultivate the practices that lead to the results that will be necessary for us to get there. If you want to embrace this shared approach and challenge, then please select me as your superintendent. I will bring these unwavering commitments as your leader."

Having distributed his corks, Jack laid out his vision for the system, the schools, the school principals, and the school staff. For the record, Jack Lowden was hired as superintendent and provided leadership for that district for many years.

There is a set of idiomatic naval expressions that are keenly applicable to the Lowden story. They include "standing the watch" or "being on watch" and its related notion of "Not on my watch." These originate from being assigned, while onboard a ship, to serve as its "watch-keeping officer." Once designated, that officer is accountable for the ultimate safety of the whole vessel and the crew. Pointedly, it also means that by definition the assigned officer is accountable for all that occurs while "being on watch." This responsibility includes its operational reliability, accidents that occur and incompatible personnel conduct in word or deed that require your intervention. Recall that for Jack Lowden, though he never cited the naval expression, he laid out clearly that on his watch and among his would-be administrative team, principals are the "watch-keeping officers" of their schools. Lowden also defined what operational reliability would mean in his system. Principals would be accountable for improving schools with improving levels of staff performance. There would be no corks on his watch.

I strongly urge you to take on this level of accountability. What happens "on your watch" is your responsibility. So, take a moment and consider these questions rigorously.

> ### Essential Questions for Your Watch
>
> *What kind of school is yours – improving, declining, or in some ways adrift and going nowhere? Do you have any "corks?"*
>
> *Are there instances of underperformance and dysfunction occurring that compromise your school's inherent and aspirational commitment to equitably and effectively serve all students and families?*
>
> *What signals may tell you that your school is adrift?*
>
> *Metaphorically, or perhaps urgently and in reality, are there accidents waiting to happen that you can and should stop?*
>
> *Are words or deeds in use among your staff, students, or community that are incompatible with your developing an improving school or that are indicative of early warning signs of its imminent decline?*

Principals, it is on your watch that the norms to influence and improve your schools will be created and sustained. You are responsible for interrupting any declining performance, and for catapulting your school toward new and lastingly positive results. To conclude these metaphors, if there are patterns within your school contributing to its being adrift like a cork on a nowhere sea, or if there are members among your staff who are adrift like corks, you are accountable for helping them to sight a new lighthouse on your watch. Your ship, that is to say, your school must not scuttle against shores of underperformance or dysfunction. Preferably on your watch, you and they will embrace collective responsibility and chart a course toward destinations of compelling and visionary choice. There will be no corks on your watch.

What's Going on Around Here?

As a principal, how would you answer these questions: "What is it like to be a student learning in the classrooms of your school? How do teachers engage students and with what ends in mind? Do students participate in inquiry and research? Do they create original work products to demonstrate or represent their personal understanding? Do they experiment? Do they publish using mixed media? How frequent are student-to-student interactions? Are learning experiences generally consistent across class-rooms? Are they of similar high quality? How do teachers assess student learning? In short, what are students asked to do and for what purposes? What are your school's patterns and what are its exceptions?

Whether you are a principal newly appointed to your school or one who has had many years of service there, there may be no more critical questions for your leadership. These go to the heart of what quality, equity, and learning mean for each learner in your school. Furthermore, your answers to these questions may vary over time, based on a host of factors such as the time of school year, professional development, staff retention or turnover, and externally imposed district or state requirements. Finally, **because your principal's imperative is to elevate your students' learning beyond their current levels of performance, how will you determine where to begin that quest?**

As an opening disclaimer, please be assured that I truly believe students benefit from having different kinds of teachers and experiencing various teaching styles. For example, some teachers possess gifts in illuminating great writing or modeling inspired authorship. Some may be more entertain-ing, theatric, and dramatic storytellers. Others may be more provocative, stimulating students to explore and debate real-life issues from many per-spectives. Some may be very emotive and personal, evoking humanistic and multicultural connections. These variations and differential nuances among teachers may be endless. So again, I acknowledge in this truth how teachers' unique gifts can provide students with life-transforming benefit.

In the end, though, I submit that it is insufficient for principals to celebrate and support teachers' uniquely delivered gifts. For at every level within the PreK-12 spectrum, principals are responsible for the quality and equity of outcomes. This is true among both students and staff.

Thus, as principal, I ask you to ask yourself these questions:

> *What are my "bottom line" expectations for teaching and learning in my school?*
>
> *What does every student deserve within the learning experiences of my classrooms?*
>
> *How is it working in the classrooms of my school now?*
>
> *How must it work in my school's desired future?*

Again, let me introduce another disclaimer before proceeding further. Later in this volume, we will focus intently on how principals can and should engage their staff in developing shared answers to such questions. However, for now and always, please recall and understand Jack Lowden's earlier point. Principals are each school's "watch-keepers" and as such, what happens in your classrooms will always be "on your watch."

Nowhere is this point more evident than when we consider your school's curriculum. Are the written, taught, and learned curricula the same from classroom to classroom and subject to subject? Are teachers supported and challenged to be responsible for providing that curriculum with any universally implemented principles of practice? Do you make it clear that whether a student is in your first-grade class, in your 7th-grade science class, or in your 10th-grade social studies class, he or she must be assured of and have access to a certain quality of teaching and learning? Furthermore, are these associated with accomplishing a set of articulated standards-based outcomes? Thus, in your school, do you support capable teachers' differential teaching as an enhancement to a commonly assured learning curriculum? Or does your school function as a more loosely coupled set of classroom learning experiences? Is student learning more variable from student to student and teacher to teacher? Or is it more consistently referenced and equitable in its access to common outcomes?

I assert that while capable and differential teaching is expansive and exciting for your students and their families, loosely coupled teaching that yields inequitable outcomes is unacceptable. ***It is vital to distinguish a teacher-originated classroom that you may permit by default from the teacher-enhanced classroom that you support within coincident expectations.*** The former denies students their promise to have equitable access to valued learning outcomes. The latter fulfills your responsibility to ensure valued learning outcomes for every student.

A 30-Day Scan

So, you're the principal. ***How do you know what's going on in your school? On what basis do you know what's working and what is not in the classrooms of your school? I advocate you undertake a periodic 30-day scan of your classrooms utilizing any of a variety of high-frequency visitations.*** Three specific techniques are introduced and modeled below. With these, you gather observational and other qualitative evidence about the nature of teaching and learning in each of your classrooms (as well as educational service settings). This data enables you to have the basis for making broader generalizations about your school.

When I was a school system superintendent, scanning was part of my orientation for and collaboration with new principals hired to join our system and become new members of our schools' leadership team. I asked them to complete a 30-day scan within the first four to five weeks of the school year (or their entry date if it was mid-year), and then return to review with me what they had learned about teaching and learning at their school. In fact, I also told them that as new hires, they were a valuable new resource for the rest of our principal team and me. Their fresh set of eyes and classroom observations when aggregated as a 30-day summary offered me and us new insights both about our schools and our learning curriculum. However, it also afforded me a collaborative opportunity to converse with that specific new hire directly and to support their developing and initiating a set of plans for working with their new faculty. Imagine, then, that I am replicating that collaborative preparation and process here, enabling you to undertake 30-day scans as a foundation that you might choose to undertake with your staff at your school.

Visitation Technique One

Scripting is the first tool among your scanning and visitation techniques, and it is much heralded and documented in the educational research literature. I have seen it used in two ways. First, during individual principal's regular classroom "walk-throughs." Alternatively, they can expand this process to involve teams of faculty who collaborate in conducting classroom "instructional rounds." Each is a means of observing and collecting scripted evidence and artifacts about classroom interactions, engagement, resources, and the assigned student work tasks used as a means for assessing student learning. Collected over thirty days with repeated high-frequency visits per classroom, patterns and insights may be constructed and clarified about four important aspects of classroom learning experiences. These may be aggregated across the school as a whole or even summarized within its subsegments (e.g., grade levels or departments).

In Chapter Three, we will discuss student engagement, rigor, and complexity in more detail.

Visitation Technique Two

> **Four Important Aspects of Classroom Learning Experiences**
>
> *The nature and frequency of teacher-student interactions*
>
> *The nature and frequency of student-student interactions*
>
> *The qualitative rigor of the tasks and materials associated with those interactions*
>
> *The means teachers use to have students demonstrate what they learn*

"A Day in the Life" is another interesting means for visiting classrooms and conducting your scans. While still employing scripting or your other means for observational notetaking, you schedule your visitation time and collect your observations from the perspective of what learning is like for particular kinds of students. Depending on the grade span of your school, this will occur differently. If you are a primary grade principal, you might identify reading instruction to scan at each grade level, beginning with visits to each of your four first grade classrooms. As you sit in and observe, perhaps you will discover a need for greater differentiation in how teachers are utilizing the basal reading series within each of the leveled reading groups. Your observations might reveal, for example, that among so-called "above grade level" readers, teachers are providing few, if any, enrichments to the basic reading and related exercises. Perhaps you might scan with the view of ascertaining any differential value for students receiving instruction at some grade levels within a workshop model using leveled libraries.

As a middle-level principal, you might select grade level teaming to scan, visiting each of the English, math, science, and social studies classrooms within your multiple 8th grade teams during a particular week. You might be exploring whether there is any interdisciplinary instruction occurring (one purpose for teaming). You could observe if teachers are using reading instructional techniques drawn from recent professional development presentations to increase grade-level literacy. More fundamentally, your scan might be to discern what actual instructional value results from scheduling students in grade-level teams.

As the high school principal with homogeneously grouped classes, you might "follow" single student's schedules for several or more consecutive periods for each of a low, middle, or honors designated student. Then you might reflect upon the qualitative difference of being a learner at each level. Perhaps you will discover intervention level classes akin to a trivial pursuit experience predicated upon memorizing discrete content and replicating correct procedures. Maybe as you complete scans of middle-level and honors classes, you will conclude that the only functional difference between them is that honors students do and complete more of the very same activities. Alarming is the fact that rarely do "honors" students engage in more challenging levels of inquiry or exploratory applications of content and skills.

Distilled to their essence, visitations and scans provide you with evidence. "A Day in the Life" allows you to delineate and describe the similarities and variability among your students' schooling experiences. ***More importantly, you will confront every principal's essential inquiries, "Can I support what's going on in my students' classrooms?*** Is it developmentally appropriate? Is it differentiated as needed? Is it equitably provided? Does it provide access to valued learning outcomes? Is there evidence of learning?"

Visitation Technique Three

Our final visitation technique is "Context and Closure." Two long valued and related principles of instructional design and practice are the underpinnings for these scans. I call them context (at the start of a lesson) and closure (at the lesson's conclusion). With context, teachers first clearly articulate, explain, and publish learning objectives for students. They may be posted on the board, distributed in a handout, or introduced orally. The principle of practice is that students should know what their goals for learning are in advance. For example, this may include what they are supposed to be able to accomplish by the conclusion of the task, lesson, period, unit, day, or week ahead. Each learning segment includes an anticipatory set of activities to refresh students' prior knowledge or to familiarize and model new vocabulary, concepts, and skills. In short, students have a developmental context from which to assimilate and gain access to the learning they are about to undertake.

Of equal importance to context is bringing closure to a learning sequence or set of activities. This undertaking may take many forms. Teachers highlight a lesson's essential concepts and skills, review key illustrations and models, and summarize how students may apply them to complete assigned homework successfully. Students stow materials away and set partially completed work projects aside. Teachers forecast what the predicted starting point for resumed learning activities will be when students return and forecast how they will connect to the lessons that will follow when instruction is resumed. In these many forms and others, closure activities function to provide students with developmental bridges for accommodating and synthesizing new learning with prior learning.

In brief, the point of having both context and closure for virtually every lesson experience is to provide and facilitate coherent learning for students. With designed intention, they know how to start and finish each connected set of learning sequences. In turn, they also begin forecasting how to use and apply their learning the next time.

How then does a "Context and Closure" scan work? Like other scans, artifact collection and either note-taking or scripting will be common elements for your two sets of high-frequency observations. In the first set, you will consciously scan for evidence of how teachers start their lessons and students begin their engagement. You will visit classrooms for approximately the first ten minutes of lessons over a block of days. Eventually, you will gather and filter your lesson "starter" evidence through the prism of context, organizing it into patterns using an inquiry question: "In what ways and to what extent do teachers routinely provide context for starting student learning?"

The second set of observations alternatively scans the last ten minutes of lessons, collecting evidence and organizing it into patterns about how teachers finish their lessons and students conclude their engagement in the lesson. You organize this evidence with a slightly different inquiry question: "In what ways and to what extent do teachers routinely provide lesson closure experiences for students' learning?" As is valid with other visitation constructs, "Context and Closure" allow you to organize patterns that you can view as a school-wide holistic snapshot. You can also look at it as a disaggregated depiction of grade or subject matter student groupings, or perhaps even as a comparing and contrasting of classrooms of your experienced versus less experienced teachers.

Scans are a Process and Not an Outcome

In summary, a 30-day scan relies on a very concentrated observation period that is strategic in its scope, data collection, and subsequent pattern development. The keys here are several-fold. Your scan is a high-frequency sampling, not just a series of one-shot visits. It may be either focused on particular areas of importance in your considerations or comprehensive across a spectrum of multi-grade level or multi-departmental programming. Most importantly, your scan is not designed or intended to evaluate specific personnel. Evaluation is a wholly different principal process and taken up at length in Chapter Four. ***In the end, observational scans with collected evidentiary data becomes useful to create a current and descriptive profile of teaching and learning in general, as well as to ascertain the extent to which valued principles of practice are routinely in evidence.***

Thirty days have been recommended not as an absolute number but as a means of investing sufficient time and duration to enable you to visit your school's array of teaching and programs. The 30-day scan will rely upon you allocating daily or multi-day blocks of your time. You need the opportunity to accumulate a broad set of current (and perhaps updated) evidence upon which to ascertain the current universal state of teaching and learning in your school or the depth and breadth of its variations.

The scan is not proposed as an end but as a beginning. It is a process and not an outcome. Eventually, you may choose to adapt and use scanning to be both a pre and post review of some things you and the staff are implementing. For example, using pre and post scans may help you and your staff consider, "What were our classrooms like when we started versus how students are engaged in their learning now that we are using new strategies?" ***Scanning always leads you to new inquiry. It doesn't bring closure.*** Your new questions will include at least these: "What will I do with this current evidence and its related pattern or profile? With whom shall I do so? And to what ends?"

What's Your Hypothesis?

How are you influencing the results of your school? Have you created one or more pilot projects, or together with your faculty, are you implementing a current Theory of Action? For example, is it your current hypothesis that if your faculty pays attention to certain things, does some things and not others, applies particular principles and practices, and so on, that you will learn something important that you might not know about now? Is your working hypothesis that if you do all those things, you and your staff may achieve better results than you have been able to accomplish before? Drawing upon your Chapter One role as the Preacher, have you and your staff declared a "moonshot?" The point is that perhaps you have undertaken a bold Theory of Action toward an ambitious goal, and you hypothesize that in doing so, you will be able to achieve a new and desired future for your students and your community.

I encourage you to borrow liberally from our friends in the natural and social sciences as you do your school improvement work. **As a principal who commits to school improvement, you must engage in some version of longitudinal studies.** Typically, these involve posing research questions or testing a research hypothesis. Then as discussed extensively in this chapter's previous subsection, you will employ various data and evidence gathering protocols over time. The 30-day scan uses pre and post sampling within a research question approach --- "What is teaching and student learning like in your school's classrooms? What dynamics and circumstances influence why that is so?" As you scan and observe, collect data and evidence, and then develop descriptive patterns of teaching and learning, you produce a set of time-sensitive snapshots of how your classrooms are operating. **When you repeat this process at two or more intervals within a given school year, you create a lens through which to examine how classrooms are functioning and perhaps reveal improving patterns.** You may now describe not only the changes, but also consider what conditions or factors gave rise to them. This is critical if you are going to elevate teachers' performance so that they may elevate the learning of students.

Let us consider a specific example. During the third quarter of the year, your second round of classroom observations revealed a significant shift in how teachers initiate daily instruction. You discover that more than 50% of your teachers are posing open-ended inquiry questions to commence and focus each day's lesson. This shift contrasts with your September pattern where 90% of teachers featured a list of task completion activities as the student's daily objective. You can now speculate why this might be so. Is this an indicator that student learning has matured in some classrooms and not others? Are some teachers using the fall's professional development strategies to incorporate higher-order thinking skills in their lessons while others are not? Could both perspectives be true? On the other hand, is there something uniquely evident among the continuing task-oriented classrooms? For example, are the inquiry-averse teachers the ones who are teaching their courses for the first time such that they have yet to master the curriculum themselves?

The research question approach provides meaning from your keen observations sampled over time. Be aware, though, that while valuable, it will often open further research in the form of your hypotheses and theories of action. Determining what direct and indirect variables may serve as causes for what you have observed will likely emerge from scans. Thus, hypothesis testing, coupled with your Theory of Action intended to influence outcomes, will frequently precede or follow from the exploration of research questions. In either instance, subsequent data collection becomes essential; primarily when you use these approaches in combination.

To illustrate, suppose that your faculty has committed to base each lesson plan on a particular set of relevant, content-related learning standards. Will the underlying hypothesis then prove true as a result? From classroom to classroom, will your teachers deliver a more consistently taught curriculum? Suppose the faculty has committed to increasing student engagement within classroom learning activities by shifting from teacher-led discussions toward increasing the frequency of student-to-student questioning and interactions. In theory, this shift provides teachers with opportunities to observe and monitor each student's evolving understanding and application of content and skills. However, will the increased use of student-to-student engagement prove to influence actual student learning? And will teachers use this new daily context to assess individual student's performance and growth with greater effectiveness than might have been true when they were engaging select students one at a time?

The results of your hypothesis testing will require you to do additional analysis. New research questions will almost always emerge. For instance, did every teacher plan and use the content standards you agreed to? If not, you must ascertain what it is about teaching to standards that seems viable for some staff and not others. In the new student engagement activities utilized, are all or only some teachers able to make discriminating observations about individual learning? If so, what are they doing that the others are not?

In the earlier Chapter One sections entitled *Mobilizing is Job 1* and *Moonshot Thinking*, both Rhonda Vasquez and Kasey Samuels articulated desired futures based on data-informed evidence, another kind of scan. They also set premises for collective action to accomplish new and ambitious student results. **In their cases, their hypotheses about literacy would become theories of action as illustrated to the right. You may also wish to review again pages 15 and 16.**

If I/we improve our students' abilities both to comprehend a variety of complex textual materials and to draft detailed and accurate summaries of what they have read, then student learning of subject matter content will increase across the board.

If we plan and provide the right professional development program, teachers will master and use a variety of effective instructional techniques for making text accessible and, as a result, help students to comprehend their texts. For example, these will include pre-reading vocabulary development, using guided reading strategies like "thinking-aloud" and having students make and articulate personal connections to their texts.

As a principal, you have a hypothesis when you have identified possible or desired results you wish to achieve, and you then control or shift the input variables that will influence subsequent faculty interactions among themselves, among teachers and learners, or both. Having done so, your working belief, your Theory of Action, and therein your hypothesis will project that a potential, predicted, or desired result (or set of results) will become possible. In the end, though, creating your hypothesis and acting on your theory will only be your beginning. It will be necessary, but it will not be sufficient to bring closure to your quest for becoming and sustaining an improving school. Over time, one hypothesis will spawn results that may likely give rise to another more refined or alternate Theory of Action framed within a new hypothesis. So, your surveying will continue. As I stated early on, this is a process and not an outcome.

The Surveyor

Endnotes

The Principal as Surveyor

- Takes responsibility for what is happening on his or her watch.
- Focuses on the quality and trajectory of teaching and learning.
- Uses research questions to determine what is going on.
- Scans and collects observational evidence.
- Considers what may be necessary to move toward future improvement(s).
- Charts and takes a course toward increased performance and improvement.
- Uses a hypothesis to illuminate a Theory of Action to guide collective efforts.
- Monitors progress using additional scans that will account for evolving results.
- Generates new research and new hypotheses based on evidence to develop further the conditions necessary for sustaining improvement and realizing the desired future.

CHAPTER THREE

ROLE THREE

THE DEVELOPER

THE DEVELOPER

36

Principals develop their people. You facilitate and expand your staff's capacities to perform the vital work of educating children and youth. This responsibility requires you to have intention, focus, and perseverance. To live into being the Developer is to observe, unlock, align, associate, and concentrate the attention of a veritable Rubik's cube of personnel combinations. You will consider, design, deliver, and provide guided support. You will tailor experiences to promote your staff's individual growth within their specified roles while supporting and developing a multiplicity of staff subgroups that share responsibilities.

Your Developer role also has essential underpinnings. It relies on you having established a Vision and Purpose before you initiate Action(s) for Results. No one will line up for a march with you to nowhere. You may scan for corks adrift in a nowhere sea, but you cannot be one yourself. So, you will prepare and draw deeply from the wellspring of your Preacher and Surveyor Roles. Being the Preacher will give you an articulated public voice of purpose and future destiny. It may create new intentions for your school's collective journey toward a new performance-based destination. Being the Surveyor will ground you in your current world's realities and project the topography, albeit the challenges and work ahead. In combination, you will formulate one or more hypotheses about how to evolve your school.

As the Developer, you will identify and take actions, including the provision of training programs that you (and ultimately your teachers) believe will prepare them to enable students to accomplish envisioned results. However, all this must be implemented and performed with coherence and without mystery. Development must happen in plain sight and without hidden agendas. It is beholden to and answers the questions: *"What are we doing around here? Why are we doing it? Will it get us where we need to go? How else must we prepare?"*

Finally, when you assume the Developer role, you must come off of your bully pulpit. Development is not a treatment applied to or on your staff. It is best accomplished with your people, and with you at their proverbial side. It is far more likely that a movement can begin upon a foundation of shared experience. From that wellspring, you can overcome fitful starts and sustain perseverance. In these remarks, I do not diminish the Preacher role. You will often need to convey a spirited quest to a higher calling or describe a necessary path to a new world. Frankly, your staff deserve to know your aspirations. However, they also deserve to understand and see demonstrated how their leader will share accountability. Thus, for me, ***the distinguishing work of*** *the Developer is that you will learn and toil with your staff. In addition, you will engage with staff to develop capacities for having quality discourse that will yield shared calls to action and encourage commitment to accomplishing visionary results.*

Engagement is Your Three-Legged Stool

Your principal's job has many daily demands and competing responsibilities. How have you chosen to use your time? More importantly, when considering our purposes here, how have you distributed and applied your time? After all, you know that your time is not infinite. You have everyday challenges to be efficient as well as effective in all you must do and want to do. Furthermore, front-burner issues often will intrude. Without your appropriate attention to address them, they may spawn a morass of discontent or serve to cloud any path to your aspiring school improvements.

Nevertheless, you are the principal and it is your watch. You are responsible for and must commit relentlessly to improving the quality of your school's teaching and learning. So, if we acknowledge that you do have finite time, then you must be keenly intent on how you will use it wisely and with impact. In my experience, that means focusing your attention and energy on developing three particular forms of school engagement to elevate your school's performance. These include: (1) your principal actions as taken with and among your staff; (2) actions that staff takes among themselves; and finally, (3) actions staff take with students. In practice, each of these trios influences the nature of the other two. This synergy among them is so real that if as a principal you overlook or avoid attending to any one of them, I submit that you will risk inducing a calamitous collapse to your overall improvement efforts. Said differently, defining and strengthening each form of engagement, as well as the developmental interactions among them, establishes your school's firm foundation to achieve improved, ambitious, and equitable results for all students. It is akin to you being able to stand balanced on a stable three-legged stool. Each leg is essential, and the stool boosts your ability to reach and obtain something you value that is currently out of reach.

Other esteemed researchers and educators have written extensively on all manners of creating and sustaining these three interactive forms of school engagement. Here I provide you with what, for me, has been a distilled set of transformative means to enhance each leg of your three-legged school engagement stool.

These translate into three focuses for your Developer repertoire, including:

Engage in team learning. It provides a facilitative context for developing staff.

Provide resources and means for staff to engage each other effectively as a professional community. This approach develops collective capacities for growth, problem defining, problem resolving, and collective decision-making.

Engage teachers in both instructional design and reflective practice as the pre and post processes for accomplishing active student engagement in the classroom.

Principal Engagement with Staff: Team Learning

Team Learning is an invaluable process to employ within your multifaceted role as the Developer. When you embrace and use it, you commit to regularly participating with your staff in what you may variously refer to as in-service courses, staff training, or professional development (PD) sessions. This learning expresses not less than three critical messages to your staff. First, and at the simplest level, you are willing to stop your clock and share in the learning experience. By taking part, you convey that training content is vital to you as well. It is not exclusively essential for them (even though on a day-to-day applied classroom basis, it could be). This engagement also has the immediate effect of flattening the hierarchy of your school. You are not handing down PD from on high, foisting it upon them, and having your only engagement be accounting for their attendance.

Second, once you are in the session room, you can model sincere interest, attentiveness, participation, reflection, and research. Your authentic active involvement also mitigates any lingering suspicion that you are present only to watch over the staff or to inspect its conduct. Third, by learning together, you and your team can enter into sophisticated conversations, side-by-side discussions, and actual professional inquiry. How does this fit with what we/you are doing now? How will it enhance our/your pedagogic repertoire? In what ways and to what extent would it enable us/you to engage your students even more effectively in learning? As your principal, what must I understand about the content and skills being introduced so as to support your practicing and incorporating it within your teaching?

Ultimately, team learning allows you to speak with your staff about how the session's content and objectives align with your school's articulated mission. In advance of a workshop series, for example, you might set the stage for team learning with a vision and purpose linked message like: "You and I have an ongoing responsibility to fulfill a common professional mission. We do this when we participate together in activities to serve students as well as possible. In this workshop series ahead, we will be exploring and enhancing what we know and do to engage students effectively in learning. This process is vital and is worthy of our continuing mission."

Despite the preceding advocacy, it is appropriate to raise a cautionary note. I submit that while your active engagement in team learning is a necessary dimension for you being the Developer, it may be insufficient as a sole means for overcoming typical and well-documented inefficiencies and limitations of staff development programs. Too often, they are provided as a one-shot, idiosyncratic, and disconnected professional growth experience. Consequently, and predictably, post-training use will wane or become so scattershot from classroom to classroom that any hope of equitably realized student results will be nonexistent. Usually, the supplementary infusion of high-impact modeling and follow-up coaching will increase frequent implementation and cause more individualized fidelity with intended training objectives to occur.

Last, in-service is sometimes scheduled and universally administered in mandatory "all- hands-on-deck" meetings even though they purport to present critical bodies of knowledge, procedures, or skills. Unfortunately, this too might prove counterproductive. Though admittedly, this avoids relying on staff volunteerism to acquire and use what you may deem as important or essential, without applicable interpolation of whole-group training for subsets of practitioners, its impact will likely be compromised or diminished accordingly.

All these concerning issues notwithstanding, in my experience, **when you engage in team learning, you employ an early antidote for so much of what ails typical staff development.** Within the gatherings and as you learn what your staff is learning, you can engage in concurrent conversations about the training's pedagogic applicability and make inquiries to clarify the staff's perceived needs for implementation support. You demonstrate your desire to understand and your clear commitment to using impactful instructional and assessment practices within your school. You communicate that what occurs during in-service will not stay there. You begin to overcome one-shot development because you initiate ongoing and informed dialogues through which you exchange observations about how subsequent use is proceeding. In these, you will begin and be modeling the customization process for both individuals and sets of colleagues. Team learning also offers you a favorable context to extend co-learning into interactive practice with non-evaluative feedback. You can provide and schedule such an inter-classroom visitation program using qualified substitutes or other staff. Staff volunteers may be enrolled to model and/or co-teach with each other and/or even with you.

A final consideration for using team learning is how you will commence the process. The simple approach is to just start showing up and doing what I have suggested. However, I recommend you take a prior step. Help your staff to understand your intentions for collegial engagement and your acting as the co-learning Developer you will be. To do this, reassume and borrow from your roles as a Preacher and Surveyor. Eric Jansen's principal story is instructive here. He integrated the three roles, and his staff knew what was coming in advance.

On the night before his first faculty meeting in the waning August days of summer, principal Eric Jansen sat at home pondering a range of possibilities that would both invite participation from and convey a message to his new staff on their first day back for school opening preparations. From the get-go, there was much at stake. For even as a seasoned administrator, he knew that the key to both his and the school's success would be focusing their collective energies. He didn't want to sound wonky, citing all sorts of educational research, but clearly, there was a lot about which shared professional learning would be beneficial. With books open across his desk, Internet searches abounding in his laptop browser tabs, Eric extracted and bulleted a few well-documented items along with earnest aspirations on an index card. He would use these as his talking points the next day rather than reading a scripted speech.

"Good morning," he began with enthusiastic cheer, making eye contact with as many as possible before continuing. "I am honored to be here, our first day as colleagues. What I know to be true as we begin our work together is that I now stand before the single greatest factor and resource for improving our students' achievement; more than demographics or backgrounds, more than family involvement, more than changes in curricula, rotations of textbooks, dollars per pupil, or even our class sizes.

Without equivocation, decades of educational research have told us, it is YOU the teacher - the quality of YOUR preparation, of YOUR knowledge in YOUR fields and YOUR skill in understanding and using the tools of our professional craft to enhance student learning.

Thus, as your principal, conversations with YOU will be at the heart of what we do. The future is ours to create, so let's figure out what's working and what isn't as our students strive to reach their greatest potential. Let's add new tools to our toolkits and share how they can be used to meet our students' needs. And finally, let's be ambitious and tackle what may have seemed insurmountable before.

Colleagues, we know that we have an essential purpose and that what we do makes a difference, especially when we do it well. So, I will end this morning where I began. Teaching influences learning and for this research-based fact, our whole team is responsible. I am confident that conversing and collaborating with you will be how we enable our students to achieve and succeed. I look forward to our work together. Thank you and have a great year!"

Eric Jansen engaged his staff with his first opening day speech, albeit with the first use of his bully pulpit (The Preacher – Mobilizing as Job One). Unpacking his remarks reveals his use of other principal roles. Observe how he immediately made it permissible to identify and discuss *"what's working and not working"* (The Surveyor – The Scan), *"Let's be ambitious"* (The Preacher – Moonshot Thinking), and *"to add new tools to our toolkits, and share how they can be used to meet our students' needs"* (The Developer). He forecast that as his faculty's principal, *"conversing and collaborating with you* (The Collaborator – discussed extensively in Chapter 4) *will be how we enable our students to achieve and succeed"* (The Preacher - Vision and Purpose). Their planned conversations would be *"at the heart of what we do"* (The Developer – Action).

Eric Jansen's bully pulpit address also integrated each key element for elevating school performance – Vision and Purpose (i.e., *"for this research-based fact, this whole team will be responsible"*) – Action (i.e., *"Teaching Influences learning"*) – Results (i.e., *"our students strive to reach their greatest potential"* and *"we enable our students to achieve and succeed"*). Importantly, Eric employed pronouns with precision to create an advanced context for joining in team learning and also being an authentic co-learner. Take note again of these examples: "*The future is <u>ours</u> to create; Let's (Let <u>us</u>) figure out what works; how <u>we</u> enable our students; and, <u>our</u> work together.*" Also of particular significance is how Eric laid the groundwork for the hypotheses and theories of action he and his staff would generate saying, "*Let's ... tackle what may have seemed insurmountable before*" (The Surveyor – mapping out the terrain ahead and plotting a pathway toward a desired future).

The Principal with the Staff:

"Conversations with YOU will be at the heart of what we do."

The Staff with Each Other:

"Let's add new tools to our toolkits and share how they can be used to meet our students' needs."

The Staff with Students:

"How we enable our students to achieve and succeed."

Before we transition to the next engagement area, Eric Jansen's story reinforces one last insight into your acting as the Developer. His bully pulpit speech actually contained three calls to action. Each touched systematically upon one leg of your metaphorical three-legged engagement stool. Below, we again unpack his language with examples of how he introduced his faculty to each as essential means for growing and developing together (see sidebar).

Calls to action can be declarations for how you and your staff will develop your school. As we stated early in this chapter, if you are to stand balanced on your principal's stool to reach higher results, you will need to develop the elements of successful engagement embedded within each of its legs.

Taken as a whole then, Eric Janson's lessons for us are many. He was proactive in using the bully pulpit to mobilize his staff. He forecast the scanning and hypothesis setting process they would all undertake. Finally, he introduced engagement as central to the shared work of developing both teaching and learning. These were essential precursors for his becoming a team learner within his principal's role as the Developer.

In sum, when you utilize team learning, you become an integral and facilitative participant within a collegial learning process. It becomes your principal laboratory to introduce, explore, assess, customize, and ultimately begin to incorporate new knowledge and skills within your school's professional practices. Team learning makes these purposes your school's collective enterprise and reinforces that you will be a credible co-participant in sustaining the knowledge and its impact on students.

Staff Engagement with Other Staff: Guided Discourse

As principal, virtually every word that comes out of your mouth can focus your staff on meaningful points of engagement. Each conversation presents a further opportunity for you to develop meaningful collaboration as well as to influence the direction of both individual teachers and the staff's collective efforts. The Jansen story illustrated how a principal's public language could become a foundational rock and bastion of vision and purpose that links staff and student engagement. It demonstrated how language could serve as a lighthouse for illuminating, charting, navigating, and guiding your school's professional discourse toward elevated student performance.

However, how do you go beyond the Jansen narrative, go beyond your thoughtfully prepared bully pulpit speeches, and do the development work of intra-staff engagement? Time and again in my experience, this is best accomplished using a three-part process: (1) Garner particular types of fundamental staff agreements; (2) Use discussion and inquiry guides to generate interaction and capture those agreements; and, (3) Use principles for deliberation to guide and support productive staff discourse. With this process trio, you will activate and engage staff in the indispensable conversations necessary for all of you realizing common goals, particularly those related to achieving student results.

My experience notwithstanding, simultaneously, you also will need to address or confront two likely and interactive sources for variable professional practice. On the one hand, each school often functions as a relatively unique community with demonstrable variance among such faculty subsets as its grade levels, departments, novice and more experienced teachers, general and special education personnel, and so on. Some of this may be by institutional design, with structures and services established that correspond to the developmental and age-appropriate capacities of students to learn and master certain content and skills.

On the other hand, you may observe that previously articulated expectations, disseminated innovations, school-wide policies, instructional implementations, and utilization of training are widely varied in your staff's practice as well. In some settings, they may function in a tightly defined, coordinated, and replicated fashion, while in others, they may be more loosely defined, adhered to, followed, coordinated, or replicated in practice. Your scans as the Surveyor will provide you with the observational evidence and other artifacts to identify your points of entry in reinforcing aligned training versus corralling and channeling disparate practice toward increasingly common and intentionally focused purposes. In either case, the three-part process should serve you well in differentiating your development approach.

(1) Garner Fundamental Agreements:

For your purposes here, I openly assert that your Developer role must include coalescing a set of fundamental and shared staff agreements about what professional practices work and which do not or likely will not work in elevating current levels of student performance. From your bully pulpit as Preacher, you communicate to staff both their individual and collective responsibilities for utilizing high-yield strategies that engage and develop students and will contribute to their learning. You convey your expectation that the students in your school will have equitable access to high-quality education, whatever the organizational subdivision of services or whoever among the staff is the primary provider. While you should always value and celebrate individual staff initiative and innovation, American education promises that every student deserves an equitable pathway and is equally worthy of having access to growth, development, and achievement. You cannot reserve this promise for just the students fortunate enough to have your school's most capable teachers or pupil personnel staff. The point of garnering fundamental and shared agreements then is simple. You and your staff must hold yourselves accountable for the impact of your collective performance; that is, the assumptions about and the skills with which you will engage or differentially engage all students in becoming capable and achieving learners. Using the *Principles of Deliberation* introduced below as our third staff engagement process will support your accomplishing these levels of both functionality and accountability.

(2) Use Discussion & Inquiry Guides:

Staff time for shared work is such a valuable and limited resource. As suggested here, these guides are useful template tools with which a principal may facilitate and organize staff discussions, stimulate staff thought, promote inquiry, and capture evolving reflection and research. You can tailor the guides to have staff focus upon specific topics, explore possibilities, consider particular challenges, generate potential responses, and synthesize both individual thoughts and collective wisdom. However, I do have a caution. Effective templates also include explicit directions for self-guided use and completion. This is essential.

Unless the template's tasks and intended outcomes are self-explanatory, each subset of your faculty staff will be adrift to interpret and meet your expectations at their own discretion. On the other hand, when principals explain their anticipatory purposes within clearly articulated directions, I have witnessed countless staff groups utilize discussion and inquiry guides independently, productively, and efficiently. The templates also invited more significant democratic input and as a consequence, coalesced faculty agreements, imbued actionable commitment with shared meaning and purpose, and developed impetus for collective actions.

Your proactive design and organized use of template tools also convey important messages. You underscore your vision-driven focus for school-wide professional work. You convey that inquiry and reflective deliberations will be collectively shared among all. You untether eclectic faculty subsets from their isolated perspectives and draw them into an examination of all current practices. In the end and with these processes, you will encourage research about gaps in your school's current levels of performance. This in turn will stimulate reflection about what problems of practice and learning must be addressed. Your staff will surface and illuminate their thinking, jettison and/or conjoin disparate professional practices to formulate an explicitly overt set of shared agreements. The Developer's template tools are your principal's medium for mediating the messages you wish to convey and share with your staff. Embedded with the language of your Preacher's "Moonshot" and your Surveyor's "Theory of Action," your discussion and inquiry guides may integrate and focus staff on the inquiries introduced to you in Chapters One and Two.

What is our desired future for ourselves and our students?

What is our hypothetical Theory of Action to achieve or accomplish our desired future?

Earlier, we noted that each school setting varies in its unique and relative mix of diverse and tightly coupled professional practices. Therefore, your crafting of discussion and inquiry guides are better if you prepare each relative to your local school's needs and planned use. With this point acknowledged, however, I have provided six sample templates in this volume's Appendix. They are associated with you engaging in one or more of your first three principal roles. They are prototypes for your consideration as useful staff facilitation tools. I introduce these templates to you now because each of your other three roles benefits when you apply the Developer's mindset. That is when you assume within each position how you will engage staff in all three of its dimensions: staff with the principal, staff with staff, and students with students. The key is that once customized for local use, each template has proven effective as a guide that supports collaborative or self-mediated discussion and inquiry. The appended sample templates include: A.1 - Mobilizing Questions; A.2 - Moonshot Thinking; A.3 - Shared Knowledge to Inform a Theory of Action; A.4 - Vision to Action; A.5 - From Gaps to Goals; and, A.6 - Theory of Action.

(3) Use Principles for Deliberation:

You will have taken a crucial step in facilitating your staff's development when you provide them with customized template tools buttressed with self-guiding directions for their use within scheduled professional release time, breakout meetings, or even daily preparatory periods. Sadly though, this alone may prove insufficient for engaging your staff adequately. For example, coalescing staff agreements will not happen because you've embedded mobilizing questions within your discussion and inquiry guides, however inspired they may be with your purposeful bully pulpit derived language. To increase the likelihood that your best facilitative guides will work, you must cultivate and enhance your staff's deliberative habits before or in tandem with their initial usage. You accomplish this by introducing and having them learn how to use a set of *Principles for Deliberation.*[2] These enable staff to converse productively with one another. The principles provide routines and protocols to self-manage and direct their discussions, including how to commence discourse, exchange ideas, state rationales, listen to each other, identify options, be able to advocate, and yet do all of this while suspending judgment or lapsing into counterproductive critiques and defensive posturing.

So, how do you evolve your staff's culture such that they will not only learn such principles for deliberation but also will utilize them habitually? I have seen successful principals begin by initially allocating time within their faculty meetings. They introduced and modeled the deliberative routines and protocols so that staff was able to use them to explore and identify possible solutions for actual school challenges.

---

2   This section is inspired by the work of Robert J. Garmston and Bruce M. Wellman in The Adaptive School – A Sourcebook for Developing Collaborative Groups (Christopher-Gordon Publishers, Inc., 2009).

Essentially, these successful principals engaged staff in a series of "proof of concept" experiences that demonstrated how the new deliberation principles were possible to learn quickly and serve as practical means for the principal and staff to address both real concerns and highly charged issues. Most importantly, as these deliberation principles became more habitually employed protocols to support school-wide discourse, successful principals had effectively fostered and developed shared leadership for shared inquiry to accomplish shared results.

When Peter Thompson became the principal of his average-sized urban high school, it had a long and entrenched history of stubbornly sustained issues. Graduation rates were below all regionally comparable averages, and among the school's diploma candidates, college acceptances were very limited. Student absenteeism, dropout rates, and school-related violence were all high. Recruiting and retention of teachers was a persistent challenge. The school's student body was disproportionately diverse, composed of a majority of minorities who were, by and large, economically disadvantaged. About a decade earlier, the school's community context had further exacerbated these demographics. A significant "white flight" exodus occurred when the area's major high-end manufacturing and research employers closed and moved their operations to other more distant suburban communities.

Undaunted, Peter began his tenure with an ambitious goal and a mantra he would repeatedly assert, "Together, this staff and this community are going to help our school become an achieving one for all kids." He commenced immediate and pervasive staff conversations, focusing their attention and their deliberations on becoming able to identify issues, to nominate and sort through optional responses, to develop plans for overcoming obstacles and to resolve problems along the way. However troublesome the issue or potentially bizarre a nominated solution may have seemed it was not to be dismissed or taken off the table. Every idea was explained and considered.

Peter reached out to parents, local religious leaders, and community members as well. This expanded the school-based dialogue and engaged them collaboratively to make problem-solving and problem-resolution a school-community reality. It ceased being a historical exception. Perhaps the best example of Peter's process evolved

> *from one of the many nominated ideas. When first considered, it had been tantamount to declaring a local moonshot. It required being undeterred by the initial realizations that no current set of strategies were in place to accomplish all that would be necessary. Nevertheless, the nominated and then adopted idea became one of the school's central goals for students. Simply stated, it was that all students would apply to and receive acceptance into either an associate or undergraduate college program, or they would enroll in a post-high school career-training program. It would take five years, but Peter and his school-community accomplished this goal.*

Peter Thompson and his staff took on one of his school's real issues. Over time and within ongoing conversations, Peter's staff culture evolved from one that had tolerated students' poor performance to one that had achieved unprecedented student results. Peter's methodology was one of guiding staff and community discourse within an organized two-part conversation process. First, he got all the ideas out on the table for everyone's consideration. Then he took on the second process of selecting or prioritizing from among the alternatives.

Not unlike Peter Thompson's approach, the staff discourse process I am advocating has two phases. Each serves a specific purpose and seeks to achieve a particular goal. Generally, staff engage in each phase sequentially, because the first phase generally serves as a foundation for what is considered in the second phase. The integrity of each phase and the relatively seamless transition between them is best supported by some commonly utilized routines and guidelines.

Overarching Routines for Commencing Each of the Two-Phased Discourse Process

1. Identify a process facilitator among each group of participants engaged in the deliberations. For example, this can be the principal in a whole group meeting, or a colleague nominated from within a smaller staff subgroup. The facilitator also serves to enable and accomplish the next two routines below.

2. Announce in which phase participants are currently engaged. Help the group understand its use of time, clarifying when each phase is to commence and when it is time for closure.

3. Review and remind participants of the unique routines and guidelines they are to use while conversing during each phase. This is discussed more below.

4. Seek a volunteer to act as the recorder of the group's thinking and the scope of its deliberations. Utilize chart paper or provide a blank discussion guide to record the group's thinking. It will be valuable to capture and preserve the proceedings from each of the phases.

Phase One - The Generating Phase

The desired results or purpose of Generating is for all participants to bring to the surface their depth and breadth of thinking about a subject. It is not to pick each idea apart. Participants offer and nominate a wide array of ideas, possibilities, approaches, and solutions for consideration. They strive to support each other's understanding of each thought with clarifying questions as may be necessary to encourage further explanation or the offering of examples.

The Generating Phase engagement guidelines include:

Every participant may contribute and is encouraged to do so.

Every participant's idea is accepted for consideration.

Facilitators illustrate the kinds of responsive commentaries participants should avoid as colleagues introduce their thoughts. Examples might include: "Who's going to pay for that?" or "Yeah, that will never work."

Questions may be asked, but only for purposes of allowing the contributor to create greater clarity or understanding of the idea or the input. It should never be a grilling of the contributor to prove that their idea is viable or has merit.

The contributor may advocate for his or her input during the discourse, but the language used must be self-disciplined. It should articulate only how the input relates to accomplishing the goal or addressing the issue at hand.

Phase Two – The Evaluating Phase

By contrast, the desired result or purpose of Evaluating is to make a well-considered choice from among alternatives based on an analysis of each contributed idea. The focus of evaluative deliberations is to come to closure by vetting each Generating Phase alternative thoroughly to determine the idea, course of action, or solution deemed best from among them or from their synthesized hybrids. Necessarily then, the Evaluating Phase operates quite differently. Participants appraise each nominated idea using a variety of two-dimension assessments. In the vernacular, we might call this process one of weighing the pros versus the cons, the upside v. the downside, the costs v. the benefits, the advantages v. the liabilities, and finally, the potential positive results v. the potential negative consequences.

The Evaluating Phase engagement guidelines include:

Every participant may contribute and is encouraged to do so.

Participants explain the pros and cons of each contributed idea in relation to intended goals or desired results.

Participants seek to gain clarity about why those are the pros and cons, including elucidating and articulating such considerations as:

> *Who may be positively and/or adversely affected;*

> *What the costs and benefits of investing available resources may be;*

> *Assessing whether the requisite resources, including perceived personnel and organizational readiness, preparation, deployment, and impact, can be addressed and accomplished within a perceived necessary timeframe.*

> *Whether there are adequate measures to determine if a particular idea or alternative can be or has been successful in addressing the area of school growth or development under focus.*

Participants may also use group protocols for choosing among the alternatives. While this volume will not provide a comprehensive listing and clarification of such protocols, two processes may be illustrative.

> *In the first approach, the facilitator can provide each participant with a fixed number of binding "votes" (perhaps one's top three alternatives).*

These would be cast by show of hands. When aggregated, the votes should narrow the field of alternatives, and the process would continue (i.e., top two options and/or top alternative voting) until there is a clear majority advocacy for a particular option.

A second process provides each participant with small colored sticky notes (red for elimination – I recommend we cease further consideration of this alternative given the severity or scope of particular concerns; yellow - for caution - I have some real concerns about proceeding with this alternative; and, green - for support - I can live with and advocate this choice without reservation). Given the group's discussion of pros and cons, each participant then assigns a sticky note to each posted alternative with the color representing his or her perspective: Cease consideration and eliminate (Red); Select with caution (Yellow); or, Support unequivocally (Green). This second approach allows the group to surface both visual and verbal patterns among the group's thinking, and through conversation and explication, to further clarify whether the group can come to a consensus agreement on the relative merits of a particular alternative. Through participants' interpretation of both points of concern and/or advocacy, I have witnessed whole groups persuaded to move from red to green or vice versa, as well as initial yellow caution perspectives shifting to become the prime advocates as a green and selected option.

The second approach stands in contrast to the first procedure that relies on a strict voting protocol with a potentially selected alternative emerging solely on having at least a majority of the participant's support. In my experience, I have seen the second protocol utilized as a stand-alone process or as a means for "breaking a tie" among top vote-getters in the first voting-oriented protocol.

Having laid out the distinct purposes of the Generating and Evaluation Phases, it is essential for the staff to have universal and habitual group interaction principles to self-govern and protect each participant's opportunity to add and make clear their thought contributions within the engagement processes of each phase. These principles may be posted or distributed for reference during a deliberative discourse session in either phase. These universal and habitual Principles for Deliberation, include:

Universal Group Interaction Principles for Each of the Two-Phased Discourse Process

Focus your comments and contributions within the guidelines and purposes for each phase (e.g., generating and clarifying possibilities/ alternatives, using questions to understand and not to challenge; or, explaining and assessing the pros and cons of alternatives).

Assume each contributor's comments to be of equal value and offered with positive intentions related to the purpose of the conversation. This diminishes the possibility of negative overtones or oblique critique slipping into the discussion.

Listen attentively for the essence of others' contributions. Ask about and clarify others' thinking before initiating your own. For example, ask for greater specificity or possible examples of a point: "Which colleagues in particular?" or "Could you offer some potential illustrations of that?"

After listening and before speaking, give yourself time to think and summarize what you have heard. This also allows others to assimilate or accommodate others' comments in their thinking.

Restate or rephrase what you have heard so that the other contributors may acknowledge that you have understood them, or perhaps have the additional opportunity to clarify a missing element or interpretation of their input.

When offering ideas, consider introducing relevant information, temporal factors, or statistics with which your listeners may assess your contribution and relate it to that of other contributors. For example: "Unlike a few years ago, fifty percent of our current staff are new to our school, so we may need to …" or "There are 15 weeks left until our deadline; perhaps we should lay out a week-by-week plan to …." or "Last time I checked, only twenty percent of our parents came to our fall open house. What is our thinking about that?"

Use connective and transitional phrases when relating your input to that of others, or when seeking to synthesize two or more points. In this way, you signal what your intentions are to both reference and include their input. For example: "To build upon Bob's thought ...." or "Another consideration related to Linda's point might be ...." or "Connecting the dots among Susan's, Gene's and Eileen's comments, they each are focused on x, y and z and maybe that's our real area to resolve here."

To summarize, as principal, you can do much in advance to increase the likelihood of your staff engaging each other in constructive and deeply considered conversations. You can prepare and empower your staff to collaborate, share their thinking and experiences among each other, come to an understanding about their exchanges, and coalesce common agreements using intentional, facilitated, and often self-governing processes. These include:

Focusing the goal(s) for staff collaboration and discourse with publicly articulated vision and purpose;

Introducing and having staff use interactive tools like question and inquiry guides, commonly understood and practiced routines and guidelines we have named Principles for Deliberation; and,

Differentiating the purposes of individual staff contributions within distinct conversational segments that I have identified as the Generating and Evaluating Phases.

Staff Engagement with Students: Design and Learning

The quality and nature of how your staff engages students substantially alter their learning experiences from lesson to lesson and classroom to classroom.[3] Simply said, staff-student and student-student engagement provides an essential gateway to and pathway for students' learning and staff's assessment of that learning. When considered over an entire semester or school year, the cumulative impact of these lessons and classroom patterns can vary substantially and may already be a source of starkly different results.

---

3   This section is inspired by Phillip C. Schlechty's five forms of engagement in Working on the Work: An Action Plan for Teachers, Principals and Superintendents. (John Wiley & Sons, Inc., 2002).

On the other hand, we know from research that when students have access to and engaged with high-interest content and tasks that they perceive has value, it tends to motivate their greater investment in each learning experience. This includes their applying the necessary perseverance to understand complex concepts, master sophisticated skills, or complete exploratory projects with extended completion periods.

Thus, inherent variations among teaching will cause your students to engage in learning of their own volition, and in doing so, distribute themselves along a theoretical continuum of engagement types. The high end of the continuum is:

> *Genuine Engagement:* Students invest and become deeply engrossed in a learning activity because they perceive it has personal meaning, relevance, or inherent value. Generally, the activity also has clear goals and well-stated expectations for what is to be learned and demonstrated. However, it may also give students discretion to originate or design tasks that permit unique or collaboratively created expressions of what they understand and have considered about the content at hand.

By contrast though, as students diminish in their identification with the applicability, value, meaning, or clarity of learning assignments, or as they perceive the activities/tasks to be scripted and more directive, their engagement will likely shift and take on one or more of the following types of engagement:

> *Obligatory Engagement*: Activity completion is limited to such external rewards as getting a good mark or completing coursework one needs to go to college. This stands in contrast to the internally identified motivators of Genuine Engagement.

> *Compliant Engagement:* Activity completion is doing just enough to earn a passing grade, to "get by" and/or to avoid getting into trouble.

> *Peripheral Engagement*: Acting withdrawn, docile, and disinterested but not overtly interfering with others' learning; e.g., being present in the class but avoiding or not completing assigned activities; virtually doing nothing - putting one's head down on the desk.

> *Alienated Engagement:* Focusing one's time and energy on substitute/ alternate activities of personal interest rather than participating in or

completing assigned learning tasks; e.g., reading, drawing, gazing out the window, walking around the room, talking with another student, texting, doodling, surfing on the internet, and more.

Disruptive Engagement: Acting out, interrupting, talking out, disturbing, or defying the teacher or others during the class experience as a means of overtly not participating or complying with activity completion.

As you begin to employ this continuum, please be aware that two particular factors may give rise to individual student's varying engagement patterns and a teacher's ability to identify them. First, teachers consider and develop lesson plans in advance of instruction. These define how various content, materials/resources, and student assessments will be introduced and utilized. They further describe what student activities are intended to result in learning. Thus, staff lesson design decisions may influence how students choose to engage. Secondly, all student engagement is not alike, nor is it necessarily discernable by pure observation. To determine the form of students' engagement, teachers might need to utilize self-reporting surveys or interviews to reveal students' relative identification with or disassociation from the learning activity/task, their motivations for participating, or them having opted out altogether.

Summarily, the student engagement continuum identifies three broad kinds of student participants – more active and on-task, more disconnected and off-task, and malcontented disruptors. Setting aside the extreme disruptors as an educational intrusion deserving of both response and intervention, I may fairly caution about a potentially misleading scenario. While observable data drawn from any given lesson may reveal high frequencies of more active, on-task students completing assignments, actual engagement distinguished by being genuine, obligatory, or compliant in substance and form is not alike. Recognizing what is going on as classroom engagement may make all the difference in revealing the actual results and learning achieved within instructional activities and the data used to document it. Clearly, this relates to the 30-day scans you undertake in your principal role as the Surveyor. Your classroom visits may need to include creating opportunities to interview students without interrupting instruction or engagement.

Bluntly stated, the fact that individual students or groups of students appear to be busy, attentive on-task completers is insufficient evidence of their genuine engagement in learning. In either instance, students may be lost in either obligatory or compliant forms of engagement. The clear risk of teachers and principals drawing "false positive" conclusions regarding students' engagement is that it creates and perpetuates potential mythologies about how effective the school's teaching really is. For *"genuine engagement"* to be present, students must know what they are learning, why they are learning it, how it relates to other learning, or how it will provide access to new learning. Genuinely engaged students find personal meaning and make relevant connections. They become more able to extrapolate how their current learning will enable them to develop new understandings, consider alternate perspectives, apply skills creatively, and utilize new tools with precision or refinement.

In the end, principals who act as the Developer initiate and participate with their faculty in conversations about what student engagement is and how it influences learning. Utilizing the student engagement continuum as a resource, the discussion and inquiry will center around a series of key questions. What does your school staff know, believe, and commit to regarding engaging students? Are the current student engagement patterns in your classrooms and educational settings aligned with accomplishing your school's vision, goals, and purposes? Ultimately, what results will affirm whether your school has engaged students sufficiently well to ensure both valued outcomes and with aspirations that maximize personal growth as individual and mutually interactive learners? Thus, in your school, is student engagement effective? Is it adequate? Is it exemplary? How do you know?

However, you must anticipate that these conversations may become highly charged discussions. Setting aside the potential that some individual defensiveness is likely to arise, teachers may make a persuasive case that developing understanding and skills actually requires that elements of obligatory and compliant engagement occur first. Frankly, they may deem it as critically necessary for students to master or become skillful at using certain replicable models of composition, thought, form and function; or in designing and replicating precision-based outcomes in a plethora of applied arts and sciences. These may be important precursors to other engagement students might experience as more personally motivational such as discovering, originating, inquiring, creating, constructing, experimenting, extrapolating, synthesizing, and so on.

In my view and as illustrated with the preceding question array, seeding and facilitating your staff's discourse about student engagement must be among your highest priorities when acting in your role as the Developer. To accomplish this, you may employ the tools and resources explained in this chapter's last subsection. For instance, when provided with *discussion and inquiry guides* embedded with focusing questions and using the *principles for deliberation,* you and your staff have the means to surface shared understandings about what student engagement has been, as well as to *garner shared agreements* about what student engagement needs to become. In turn, these prior agreements become an academic foundation from which staff identifies principles of instructional practice that will promote students' genuine engagement and improved or more universally positive achievement. By contrast, the consequences of your school's not coming to closure about student engagement may exacerbate inequities and diminish performance among individual classrooms and educational service settings. Additionally, the negative impact of such an agreement void might be even more alarming among already lagging learners, including those from high-frequency at-risk youth, or demographically diverse and economically disadvantaged youth.

To integrate, your role as the Developer stands in part on the shoulders of what you accomplish in your previous two roles. As the Preacher, you will assert bully pulpit intolerance for subgroup inequities in your school and call for universal access to aspirational learning opportunities and results for all your students. You will declare your moonshot. As the Surveyor, you will scan and begin to formulate initial perspectives about whether observable variances among the teaching and learning patterns within your classrooms result in consistent, equitable and positive results for the students of your school; or whether they do not. You also will begin to formulate hypotheses about what to do next; that is, whether to sustain or to change current patterns to align future practices with accomplishing your moonshot's vision. If your hypothesis is the predicate to bold actions, your subsequent plans will frame those actions in what we referred to earlier as having one or more Theories of Action.

However, it is during the process of transitioning from scanning to hypothesis formation and the generating of related Theories of Action that the Developer will add value to staff capacities and the professional culture. You will engender the necessary deliberative skillsets for shared hypothesis formation and shared generation of Theories of Action to accomplish them. You will engage your staff in modeling, practicing, and learning how to participate in discourse using *principles of deliberation*. This approach will share your leadership by grounding the discussion in a quest to move from current realities toward the purpose of achieving shared future results. Clearly, from my experience, the number one focus for that discourse is developing shared agreement about what student engagement is and what it must become in your school. By this cycle of actions, you will demonstrate and establish shared accountability for student results among you and your staff.

Posed differently, creating a balanced three-legged approach to engagement is key to your role as the Developer. You engage your staff to develop an understanding of and to embrace a visionary shared purpose that is student-centered. You build your staff's principles and practices for deliberating to establish shared agreements that will call them to action to fulfill that purpose. Finally, you develop shared definitions of student engagement to focus on and influence the nature and quality of students' learning experiences in every classroom and educational setting. As I have modeled before, a principal's work may be translated into publicly shared essential questions to guide shared leadership and shared accountability. ***Concerning engagement, your three-part and interactive cycle of development pose these essential questions:***

> *What set of highly valued outcomes and/or aspirational results will all of our students have access to and opportunity for accomplishing in our school?*
>
> *What will be our school's Theory of Action for engaging students such that if we implement it effectively, consistently, and with fidelity, each of our students will be enabled to achieve those outcomes and results?*
>
> *What will be the quality indicators our professional team will embrace and utilize to benchmark our practices and consider their impact?*
>
> *How will our professional team assess our progress with students and discuss these assessments among ourselves?*
>
> *In using, assessing, and discussing progress measures, how will we engage each other to provide additional support as may be needed for implementing action plans or for generating mid-course corrections to them?*

Intentional Instructional Design and Reflective Practice

Over my many years of working with staff, I have distilled an interrelated set of principles, frameworks, and practices that have proven influential in motivating student engagement and enabling effective learning. These have provided a "compass" with which I have garnered shared agreements, often from within shared professional development sessions, and then provided guidance and mentored teachers during their daily lesson planning and reflections. As such, these next sections do not claim to be a comprehensive instructional primer, nor is it my intention to provide you with one. Libraries offer extensive collections of well-published authors who have addressed that task with great depth already. With that qualifying caveat, I will offer a brief series of pedagogic overviews that were both essential and useful in elevating my staff's and students' performance. For you, their value will be found in the illustrative particulars as well as emphasizing the critical importance of you having and developing your school's own academic foundation. In the end, your teachers' lesson design decisions made in advance of their teaching will influence both the quality and nature of your students' engagement as well as their learning. By implication, staff decisions made in other educational service areas will similarly be influential to those outcomes.

My point is straightforward. Intentional instructional and educational services design is an informed and recursive process for which you must hold your staff accountable. Pedagogically informed lesson design must precede lesson delivery that, in turn, provides the interactive engagement experiences and yields the assessment data for undertaking post-lesson reflective practice about results. This involves your staff conducting a realistic analysis of how well their lessons had enabled student learning, as well as reflecting upon how each lesson element had affected the quality of student engagement. Reflective practice provides essential information with which each staff provider commences their next cycle of lesson design. This recursive process is your staffs' necessary contextual crucible for engaging students in learning and achieving student results. **You are invited to examine the Lesson Design Cycle diagram and accompanying text box on page 62 which illustrate and explain these points in greater detail.**

DESIGN CONSIDERATIONS (examples):
- Lesson Goals, Purposes and Task Demands
- Student Capacities (Includes Prior Knowledge)
- Student Engagement: How & With Whom?
- School Focus: Training & Pedagogic Principles
- Relevant State & Local Learning Standards

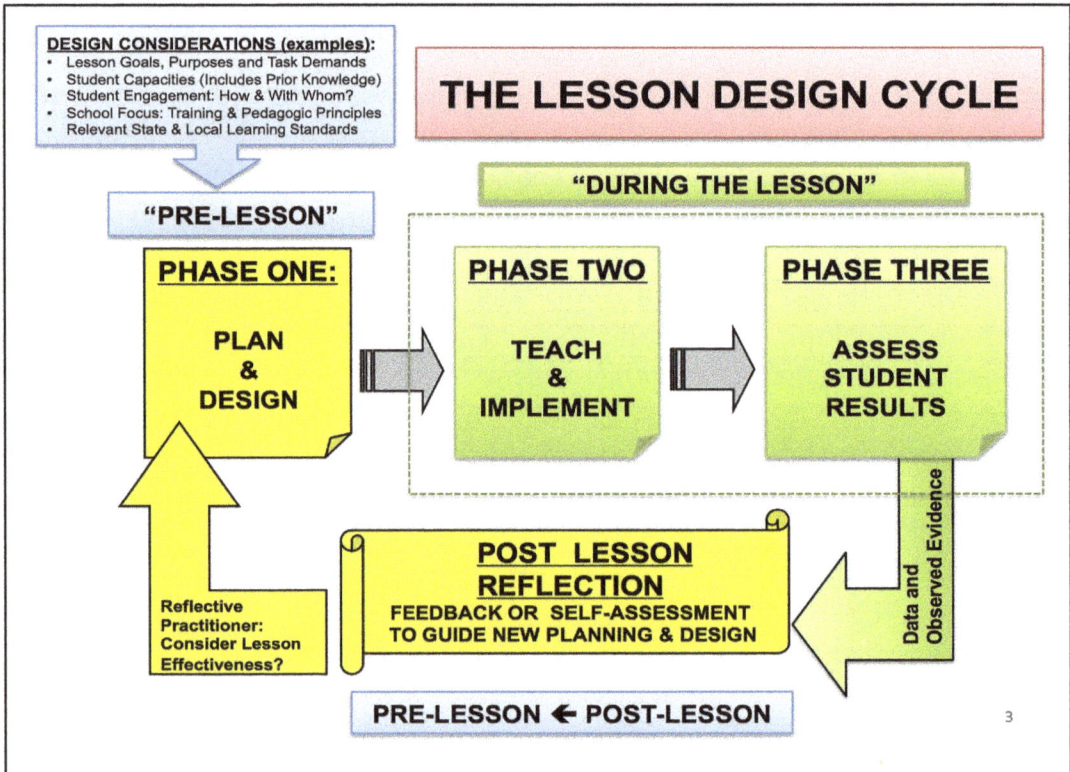

THE LESSON DESIGN CYCLE

"DURING THE LESSON"

"PRE-LESSON"

PHASE ONE:

PLAN & DESIGN

PHASE TWO

TEACH & IMPLEMENT

PHASE THREE

ASSESS STUDENT RESULTS

Reflective Practitioner: Consider Lesson Effectiveness?

POST LESSON REFLECTION
FEEDBACK OR SELF-ASSESSMENT TO GUIDE NEW PLANNING & DESIGN

Data and Observed Evidence

PRE-LESSON ← POST-LESSON

3

THE LESSON DESIGN CYCLE

Phase One teaching considers a broad range of factors to be infused as design and functional elements within Phases Two and Three. "During the lesson" teachers engage students using both resources and activities. They monitor, assess and adjust instruction to enable students to acquire skills and learn lesson objectives. Teachers embed Phases Two and Three with assessments, including: What knowledge or skills has each student learned? What is each student now able to do or apply? What progress has each student made toward a set of final goals? To what extent or in what manner were students engaged in learning designed to promote individual growth? Once student engagement observations have been identified and student results are analyzed, teachers engage in post-lesson reflective practice. They ask: (1) In what ways and to what extent did the intended lesson design and strategies engage all students effectively, and yield either expected or acceptable results? (2) What adjustments to instruction and engagement should be used to inform the next lesson's Phase One planning and design?

An Essential Role of Teaching: Being a Designer of Learning

Among the plethora of cognitive psychologists, the work of Jerome Bruner (1915-2016) and Lev Vygotsky (1896-1943), when taken together, provide powerful principles for lesson design and student engagement. Known for his *constructivist theory of learning*, Bruner calls upon teachers to design lessons that facilitate students to think originally, to discover and create connections, to construct knowledge and understanding, and to solve problems on their own. The role of the teacher is not to convey, inform, or divulge knowledge. It is to assist and make possible the student's abilities to make sense of, reason with, and find solutions among increasingly complex bodies of knowledge or problems under investigation. The teacher's role is to challenge students' learning with designed instructional supports. The teacher does not wait to engage students until the student is deemed "ready" to interact more autonomously with specific concept, skills, or resource complexities. Nor, in contrast to Jean Piaget's (1896-1980) developmental stages theory, does the teacher wait until children's cognitive development has already evolved and presumed readiness is in place for them to assimilate or accommodate the new learning with which they have been confronted or immersed. Bruner believes that it is in the very guiding and facilitating of students through newly challenging or complex material that cognitive development occurs; and that creating those challenges is part of the teacher's lesson design responsibilities. Bruner espouses creating a spiral curriculum as the teacher's means for doing so. Within this view, the teacher guides students to discover, construct, learn, and solve problems on their own by revisiting complex concepts multiple times and by gradually increasing the levels of difficulty on each occasion.

Jerome Bruner and Lev Vygotsky are linked philosophically, sharing the notion of intentionally bridging complexity within learning. Like Bruner, Vygotsky views students as having pre-existent bodies of knowledge and skills that serve as springboards for future learning. New to the lexicon were Vygotsky's concepts of *scaffolding* and the *Zone of Proximal Development (ZPD)*. Each student's pathway to future learning is via his or her unique ZPD, wherein the learning challenge is sufficiently difficult to cause and require productive struggle and cognitive growth, but is not so significant, problematic, or incomprehensible as to cause frustration and failure. It is the teacher's considerations of how to support or scaffold the student's learning that metaphorically enable the student to climb his or her individual ladder of challenge and additional complexity, to learn the new material or skill, and then to have an evolved basis for extending and applying it in the future. Like

Bruner, Vygotsky would likely counsel against matching content and ability levels precisely because of its potential for being too easy, boring, or even disengaging. However, by spiraling the curriculum and scaffolding individual learning experiences, teachers enable each student to engage productively in the learning, resulting in growth and development.

For me, the principles of Bruner and Vygotsky define each teacher's essential role and responsibility - to be a designer and facilitator of a proper learning experience. One cannot construct new knowledge or master a new skill outside the boundaries of an appropriate learning experience. Furthermore, within this synthesis, "appropriate" is defined as teachers designing and providing lessons that both challenge students at the cusp of their competence and then extend that learning with increasing levels of difficulty and application over time. It requires appropriate scaffolding. That is to say, teachers intentionally must balance supports for learning with having students engage in and experience productive, independent struggle. Within this process, they construct meaning, learn and apply skills, and demonstrate levels of proficiency, mastery, and understanding.

In practice, I advocate that as principal, you and your staff engage in a series of shared school-wide inquiries to ascertain the extent to which these lesson design principles are evident within the classrooms and your school. Examples might read as follows:

> *In what ways and to what extent are students challenged to discover, construct, learn, and solve problems on their own?*
>
> *In what ways and to what extent do students revisit complex concepts or apply newly acquired skills within experiences that gradually increase the levels of difficulty?*
>
> *In what ways and to what extent do teachers provide scaffolding to support students in constructing meaning and applying knowledge and skills, particularly in a context posing new or more complex learning challenges?*

I am pressing two key points within *Principals with Impact*. First, principals elevate school performance through discourse that garners staff agreement about those sets of pedagogic principles and professional practices that, if employed with consistency and fidelity, will most likely ensure and increase the success and achievement of all students. Embedded in that discourse is Chapter One's notion of moonshot, or what will staff success and student achievement mean around here in ways that have heretofore seemed impossible to accomplish? Together, ambitious goals coupled with focused and committed principles of practice will become the school's universal Theory of Action. Individuals and teams of school professionals can monitor the theory, assess its results, and adjust the strategies and actions being implemented. Most importantly, it becomes the common cause of intentional and resolute common purpose; i.e., to increase the school's capacities and effectiveness in elevating students' engagement, growth, success, and performance.

The second essential point is that effective lessons are designed by intention and not by default. Thus, the corollary is that student learning and success are contingent upon effective teaching that constantly improves. Given shared agreements and a universal faculty commitment to a Theory of Action, each teacher must hold himself or herself accountable for aligned and intentional lesson design. Let's be clear. I am not recommending there be an end to individual teacher creativity, initiative, or innovation. I am stating that each student deserves to learn and receive a teacher's support in achieving and succeeding to accomplish both the school's learning goals and progress along his or her pathway to future life choices after schooling. For this, principals must support each teacher in elevating his or her individual performance. It begins with lesson (or educational services) design and concludes with the process we identified as reflective practice.

Principles, Frameworks, and Practices

We have illustrated with Bruner and Vygotsky how to unpack language and reformulate essential concepts and principles into school and staff inquiries about prevalent school pedagogies and their impact on learning. The Lesson Design Cycle graphic above reveals several other sets of questions with corresponding areas of investigation to develop and influence students' capacities and their learning. As excerpted and discussed in the tables that follow, these areas are offered for their value as derived from my experience. They are not exhaustive of educational research and literature, nor are they presented as a definitive list of school-based best practices. Together, these model a principal's process and a potential set of content that, when facilitated as inquiries, enable faculties to derive shared agreements about pedagogy and practice; i.e., ***"How shall we answer this (these) question(s)?"*** The questions and their related considerations also become an array of inquiries that teachers may employ as they prepare for and design each lesson; i.e., ***"How may I use or apply this question to engage my students in this lesson/unit?"***

PEDAGOGIC PRINCIPLES, FRAMEWORKS, AND PRACTICES

Questions	Areas for Inquiry	Discussion
• What local goals, state learning standards, and curricular content define what students are responsible to learn/achieve? • Are all goals and standards equally important, or should they be prioritized within students' learning outcomes? • Will/should certain local goals or standards become universal learning targets for all students? • Should all disciplines incorporate said goals or standards within all instructional settings (e.g., literate reading and functional self-expression)? • Who will define the standard associated measures for your students' performance? Your state agency? Your district? Your school? Individual teachers? Some or all of the above?	GOALS AND STANDARDS	Often, teachers are responsible for incorporating the required content and skill standards as student learning targets and outcome goals. These requirements are developed and drawn from more external state or national curriculum or drawn from local district sources. In either instance, student outcomes are twofold: (1) To demonstrate they know about, as well as know how and when to apply/use bodies of knowledge and certain skills; and, (2) To demonstrate their knowledge and skills by meeting or exceeding defined standards with measurable levels of performance. Within lesson design, teachers must consider what content and/or skill standard(s) students are learning, how to assess students' learning, and how to define students' level of performance. Additionally, as the acquisition of knowledge and skills may require multiple lessons or extended periods of time, each lesson must be part of an intentional developmental sequence and students' progress measured and monitored over time.

PEDAGOGIC PRINCIPLES, FRAMEWORKS, AND PRACTICES (continued)

PEDAGOGIC PRINCIPLES, FRAMEWORKS, AND PRACTICES (continued)

Questions	Areas for Inquiry	Discussion
• For what purpose(s) do we expect students to learn, demonstrate, and apply their learning? Given what we know about motivating and inspiring genuine student engagement, how are our purposes aligned with engendering that objective? • At what level(s) of challenge and/or complexity are we expecting and supporting students to demonstrate their learning? • How may students be challenged at increasingly high levels? How can varying content complexity or task design contribute to doing so? • What constructs may be used within lesson designs that expect and enable students to demonstrate high levels of learning?	**CHALLENGE** **AND** **COMPLEXITY**	Teachers have access to extensive research and valuable frameworks with which to design lessons that challenge student thinking and enable them to apply skills and express understanding. While still extraordinarily relevant, Bloom's* taxonomy has been evolved and is now complemented and extended by multiple other schemas. Well-designed lessons often include leveled sets of student learning objectives using a continuum of both expected challenge and task complexity; from recalling or remembering, to describing and explaining, to using and illustrating, to distinguishing and experimenting, to arguing and appraising, to valuing and supporting, to creating and developing. Or another variation speaks to identifying, combining, and describing, comparing and contrasting, explaining causes, and reflecting, hypothesizing, or generating. Webb's Depth of Knowledge (DOK) system** uses categories to describe the levels of higher-order thinking or understanding students will demonstrate – cognitively or meta-cognitively. For example, DOK distinguishes between thinking deeply about and analyzing a task or bodies of information, with articulating how and why they would/will apply that to new situations or contexts. The expansive continuing use of text, video, media, internet-based, and other oral prompts for learning necessitates teachers' consideration of a broad spectrum of important literacy research and its impact on developing comprehension and understanding. Simply, there is an essential need for proactive introduction to meanings and usage of discipline-based academic vocabulary, pre-learning acclimation to contextualized vocabulary, differentiating accurate from inaccurate source material, deciphering bias from points of view, and comprehending meaning as derived from various literary genres and published or distributed sources of information. Finally, the applied use of Blackburn's seminal work on *Rigor**** will inform how to increase levels of complexity within student engagement. Three elements are key in her definition of the term: (1) One creates a school environment that expects students to learn at high levels, (2) Each student is supported in doing so, and (3) Each student demonstrates learning at high levels. Blackburn introduces five ways to increase rigor in learning. In brief, examples include: (a) Raising the level of content through a focus on fewer topics for depth of understanding, increasing text complexity, and creating connections through lesson units requiring applied interdisciplinary explorations. (b) Increase complexity with projects, by assessing prior understanding of vocabulary, with various writing prompts that require elaboration and explanation. (c) Provide scaffolding during reading and modeling through "think-alouds" that illustrate how to think about, inquire, evaluate, and so on. (d) Provide more open-ended questions, tasks, projects, and options providing for both greater individual investment and responsibility for personalized learning. (e) Raise expectations by having students revise and improve work rather than receive an unsatisfactory mark, illustrating that all students can challenge and learn complex new content and skills successfully.

* Bloom, B. S. (1956). "Taxonomy of Educational Objectives, Handbook I: The Cognitive Domain." New York: David McKay Co Inc.; Also - Anderson, L.W. (Ed.), Krathwohl, D.R. (Ed.), et al (2001). "A Taxonomy for Learning, Teaching, and Assessing: A Revision of Bloom's Taxonomy of Educational Objectives" (Complete edition). New York: Longman.

** Webb, N. (1997). Research Pedagogic Monograph No. 8: "Criteria for Alignment of Expectations and Assessments in Mathematics and Science Education." Webb, N. (2002) Monograph: "Depth of Knowledge in the Four Content Areas."

*** This summary is based upon Barbara R. Blackburn, *Rigor is NOT a Four-Letter Word, 3rd Edition*. (Taylor & Francis, 2018)

PEDAGOGIC PRINCIPLES, FRAMEWORKS, AND PRACTICES (continued)

Questions	Areas for Inquiry	Discussion
• What does it mean for a teacher to provide a lesson context that is "at the cusp of a student's competence"? • How is scaffolding instruction essential for developing learning within a student's Zone of Proximal Development (ZPD)?	ASSESS COMPETENCE	Assessing students' knowledge and skills is an expected element of appropriate lesson design. Bruner and Vygotsky imply that students will develop cognitively and construct knowledge from among a series of engagements, some more effective than others. Something too easy and fully within current knowledge and skill competencies may neither interest nor motivate students' engagement. Something too hard or demanding may frustrate or cause students to fail to develop the necessary capacities for constructing new skills and knowledge. On the other hand, the "sweet spot" of lesson design is a level of challenge that teachers support with intervention, modeling, and instruction that accesses students' prior knowledge and guides their skills in the process of bridging, connecting, constructing and applying at the new levels of competence. Such teacher "scaffolds" do not require students' functional independence in the face of challenge; rather, the scaffolding serves to collaborate with students in generating advanced understandings and increasing more diverse application of skills.
• How may teachers intentionally design and differentiate lessons that will provide appropriate learning experiences for all?	SCAFFOLD LEARNING DIFFERENTIATE INSTRUCTION	For teachers, however, two daily realities must be overcome. Within one classroom there are often many current levels of competence and secondly, these differences may shift or be magnified depending upon the content, resource, modality, standard or instructional goal being addressed. As a result, teachers must consider and then design each and every lesson for at least three groups of students - the Prepared, the Not Yet Prepared and the Already There. This need to differentiate instruction is a shifting but ever-present constant. The variables at the teacher's design discretion are to vary the content (What students will learn?), to vary the engagement (How students will learn, including the choices, resources, and activities?), and/or to vary the assessment (What artifact or result will be produced to determine that each student has learned)? Intentional plans that differentiate support for students of diverse abilities is the starting place to scaffold all instruction.
• How may teachers embed and integrate dispositions for learning within their ongoing mandate to design appropriate lessons? • Are there approaches for directly teaching and modeling dispositions for learning that will scaffold learning for students when they are most challenged?	DISPOSITIONS FOR LEARNING	Costa and Kallick's *Habits of Mind** collaborations provide a richly described set of learner temperaments and outlooks that are not curricular learning standards or pedagogic engagement strategies. They are an exposition of what it takes to be a learner and to succeed at learning. It is an explication about how to develop the capacities for learners' self-awareness, invest in, and sustain their learning. Costa explains how and why these dispositions must be taught and developed as a holistic learning program. Of keen interest is his recurring theme that illuminates what learners must do when they struggle to learn, and the path to understanding is unknown to them rather than when it is known and clear. What is the learner's means for achieving breakthrough? How does a learner persevere in a context of confusion and struggle? Costa's is a blueprint for helping teachers to develop students' reasoning, insightfulness, creativity, and craftsmanship to resolve complex problems, including their learning. For teachers as designers of learning experiences, Costa's framework defines teaching responsibility and efficacy on a different plane. The role of a teacher is as a developer of learner capacities to understand who they are as learners and how they can accomplish breakthroughs to learning when challenged. This expands teaching to being more than purveyors of content learning and academic skill sets. Teachers become developers of people.

* Arthur L. Costa and Bena Kallick, *Learning and Leading with Habits of Mind*, (ASCD, 2008)

PEDAGOGIC PRINCIPLES, FRAMWORKS, AND PRACTICES (continued)

Questions	Areas for Inquiry	Discussion
• How might teachers embed social-emotional competencies within their ongoing mandate to design appropriate lessons? • Are there approaches for directly teaching and modeling social-emotional competencies that will scaffold learning for students when they are most challenged?	**SOCIAL AND EMOTIONAL LEARNING**	Each teacher's development of students includes responsibility for engendering both academic and social-emotional competencies. Among others, these latter competencies include cooperation, assertiveness, responsibility, empathy, and self-control. Teachers who account for social-emotional learning create classroom cultures that honor human interaction and individual dignity, assign personal responsibility for mediating one's individual behaviors, and models and converses about appropriate personal and collaborative learning. One construct for developing such classroom cultures is known as *The Responsive Classroom** and I encourage schools to research it, engage in its training, and implement its practices as part of routine lesson design and delivery.
• How may teachers and students utilize technology and virtual resources to enable and individualize learning?	**BLENDED LEARNING**	Within obvious constraints of individual home and school budgets, students and teachers have more or less ubiquitous access to technology, virtual learning resources, cloud sharing tools and collaborative video conferencing platforms. These will continue to influence how teachers design, deliver and facilitate learning. They will also transform how students access content, interact with each other and engage with their teachers. Central to this process will be how teachers identify and adapt "blended learning" approaches that work for your school, classrooms and students. "Blended Learning is a model that combines online and face-to-face learning spaces, activities and experiences ... Courses are taught both in the classroom ... and at a distance ... It is also referred to as reverse teaching, flip teaching, backwards classroom or reverse instruction .... It could be argued that there are thousands of types of blended learning varying by content, scale, technology, learning spaces, etc." ** Teachers assign learning tasks that students complete at home or in other settings in advance of other interactive learning engagements. The classroom setting becomes a teacher's facilitative forum. They explicate learning concepts and vocabulary, as well as model necessary skills with which students will complete individual exercises or engage in group activities. By adding station rotation in its many forms, teachers plan and facilitate lesson segments as students move among small groups, guided software and digital content, differentiated individualized support, independent assessments, text reading and/or hands-on activities. Blended Learning is a powerful lesson design and delivery construct with which teachers may balance supports for learning with having students engage in and experience productive, independent struggle. Within this technology enhanced process, students may construct meaning, learn and apply skills, and demonstrate levels of proficiency, mastery, and understanding.

* *The Responsive Classroom* @ www.responsiveclassroom.org.
** https://www.teachthought.com/learning/12-types-of-blended-learning/

Engagement Summary

To conclude, developing the scope and nature of engagement within your school is a critical role for school principals. As described with the image of a three-legged stool, you must balance your many ongoing principal responsibilities with intentionally developing three sets of daily school engagement: (1) the principal with staff, (2) faculty with each other, and (3) staff with students. This will require you to draw systematically upon both the Preacher's prior moonshot thinking and the Surveyor's scanning and observations to generate hypotheses and theories of action with your staff. As a Developer, you will participate in team learning to expand your staff's universe of professional understanding and practice. This will provide developmental context to introduce and model principles and processes for deliberative staff discourse, inquire about pedagogic research, and garner fundamental agreements including a common definition of student engagement.

THE DEVELOPER

Capacity and Commitment:

A Differentiating Analysis Framework

Let's assume you have one or more working hypotheses about the set of essentials that will likely impact teaching and learning positively. Let's also assume that based upon them, you and your staff are in the midst of implementing theories of action to elevate your school's performance subsequently. Who among your faculty possess the necessary knowledge and skills to provide those essentials at high levels of quality in their classroom or educational settings? Additionally, how many of them are committed to doing so and apply those essentials with consistently high frequency? In general terms, experience has taught me (and probably you as well) that the answer to these questions is simple to state but portends a great focus for your substantial principal's work as the Developer.

First, garnering shared agreements is only your first step. Your proverbial rubber will meet an inevitable road. *On your journey to evolve and elevate collective future professional practice, you will need to motivate and sustain staff commitment to the shared hypotheses and the actions that are deemed necessary to accomplish the school's vision.* Second, the likely facts are that your school staff will vary in both their initial and ongoing capacities to commence and implement particular lesson design and classroom learning approaches equally well, particularly among a student body of diverse abilities and needs. Thus, an essential aspect of your Developer role is to undertake an analysis of these two dimensions, knowledge/skill and commitment/action.

This is an example of how your Developer Role evolves from and subsumes your earlier scanning within the Surveyor Role. You must gather evidence about and apply the two dimensions as a means for describing the individual and the collective implementation patterns among your staff. Each dimension and ultimately, each teacher, should be considered in reference to your shared agreements, especially as they are related to your overall purpose of elevating student learning and performance. Then, with the descriptive perspectives generated by your analysis, you will determine and provide the necessary development and differentiated support to enable your staff to engage each other and their students in manners aligned with the visions, purposes, and intended outcomes of your shared agreements. For the balance of this chapter section, I have provided an extended explication of a quadrant-oriented analysis framework with which to begin your differentiated staff development work. The four-quadrant analysis process works. I have supported and coached principals to use it and create uniquely considered development plans for their schools.

As you examine the graphically represented framework on the opposite page, take particular note of the four color-coded frequency levels drawn from the key and the four quadrants identified by number. The graphics also draw upon my previous discussion that when principals work with staff to identify hypotheses and theories of action, they do so to identify specific actions that will influence student learning and elevate student performance results. Thus, the two graphical axes provide parameters and scaling to denote the extent to which an individual staff member is implementing those actions with knowledge, skill, and efficacy. For example, a "5X5" Quadrant 1 teacher would be one who demonstrates the highest levels of knowledge, expertise and effectiveness in implementing those specific actions "most of the time" (i.e., with greater than 90% frequency on both ends of the "High" or "Highly" labeled axes). By contrast, observations of a "5x5" Quadrant 3 Teacher would have revealed the least knowledge, skill, or effectiveness for implementing the desired action(s) AND that he or she virtually never implements them (i.e., with greater than 90% frequency on both of the Limited portions of the X and Y-axes).

To illustrate the plotting of individual teachers using the quadrant matrix, suppose your school has committed to the prior teaching of academic vocabulary to enable rigorous student learning of particular content or as a predicate for applying specific skills. As principal, you would observe that your Quadrant 1 teachers are highly capable and committed to doing so routinely, as evidenced by both their lesson design systematically preparing for that purpose and their subsequent lesson delivery. As a result, rigorous content and skill learning is evident in these Q1 classrooms in a couple of potential ways. First, in oral discussions, students are demonstrating their comprehension of complex homework texts and reference sources embedded with that vocabulary.

Second, perhaps they are actively using skills that had been modeled and explained with task-specific functional vocabulary. Additionally, these Quadrant 1 teachers have used the prior teaching of academic vocabulary as a necessary scaffolding at the cusp of learning or competence for both independent student work and for supporting those who are less capable of mediating and comprehending texts for understanding. By contrast, a Quadrant 3 teacher is neither particularly capable of teaching academic vocabulary to enable student learning, nor does that teacher ever actually do so. The resulting impacts on students of these diametrically different teacher profiles should be obvious. It illuminates educational inequities of the highest order, with the Quadrant 3 teacher, through incompetence and/or resistance, denying his or her students access to the understanding and learning the Quadrant 1 teachers are accomplishing.

STAFF ANALYSIS FRAMEWORK

This framework is a recording and classification tool. When completed, it creates and depicts a holistic scatterplot of your entire staff. It begins by identifying your analysis of each staff member's relative position within the four-quadrant matrix. The variables of analysis are correlated with the two axes and the Key. The analysis lens for each staff member's plot point is referenced against a school's **THEORY OF ACTION** to achieve specific student results. This is represented in the question:

"What actions if taken or principles of practice if used
with consistency, will achieve our desired results?"

The X-axis assesses each staff member's actions as measured by his or her frequency in implementing those specific lesson design constructs or principles of pedagogy to which the school has committed for elevating student results. **The Y-axis assesses** each staff member's levels of knowledge and skill for effectively applying those same constructs or strategies. **The related plot point (X,Y)** will place each staff member in one of four quadrants. After plotting each staff member's data point on this same quadrant grid, a school-wide distribution pattern will be depicted regarding the Theory of Action element(s) being implemented frequently and effectively.

SEE APPENDIX – TEMPLATE A.7 for a full-scaled version of this framework.

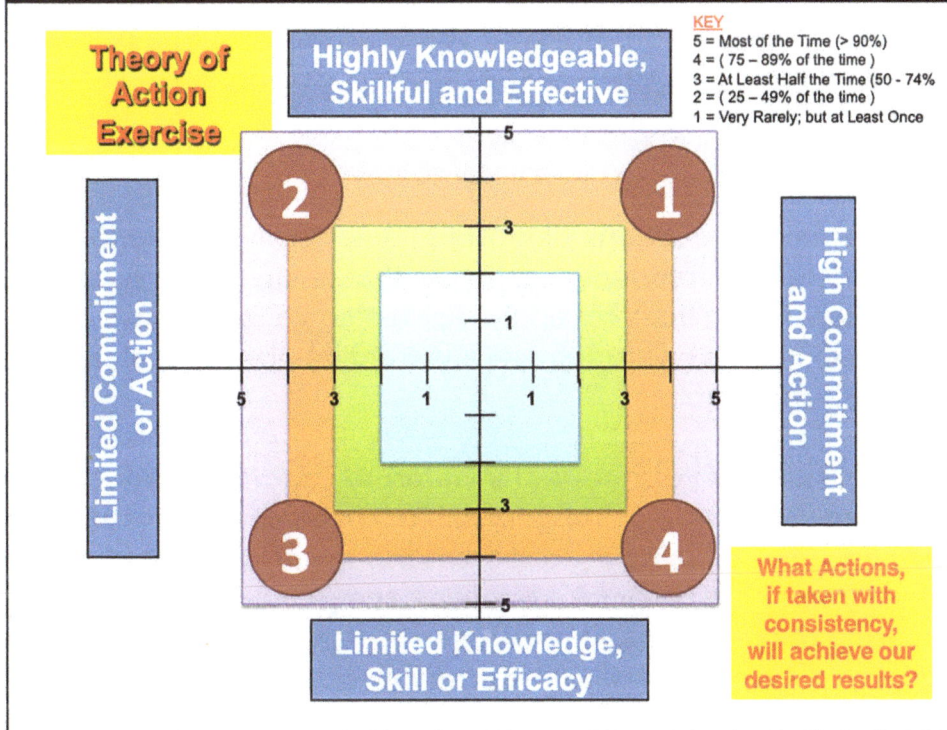

In summarizing this illustration, I want to refine further how to use these scaled axes and the quadrant analysis framework. For simplicity's sake, I have often referred to Quadrant 1 teachers who are highly skilled and demonstrate high efficacy as routine implementers of valued initiatives as "Top Guns" (with a nod toward the movie of that title). Said differently, if your faculty were a naval air squadron, your best Q1s would be your "Blue Angels," the team of expert pilots who fly in splendidly precise formations with common performance goals. As a shorthand, I have denoted Quadrant 3 teachers as "Dropouts," as evidenced in their patterns of resistance, non-compliance, and possible incompetence in integrating school-identified theories of action.

Of course, these shorthand labels are applicable only as they play out and apply to the pedagogic processes of a particular Theory of Action (e.g., the prior teaching of academic vocabulary). If we substituted "implementing Blended Learning" for "teaching Academic Vocabulary" in our illustration, the same two teachers could end up in exactly opposite quadrants. The former Quadrant 1 teacher may prove to be technology-phobic and function as a Quadrant 3, resisting or refusing to provide technology-enhanced learning experiences. By contrast, the former Quadrant 3 teacher's classroom may be a superbly effective model of using station rotation activities and of how to integrate guided software resources with diagnostic assessments among those learning stations. Perhaps the Q3's error has been that his or her over-reliant commitment to software-driven teaching has made no compensation for the fact that the technology resources currently in use do not address academic vocabulary in the textual materials also required for other assignments.

The implications and cautions of plotting individually functional teaching using dual-referenced frequency scales are that doing so is only a snapshot. It is not permanent and does not apply to all dimensions of a particular teacher's teaching or impact on students. A quadrant label is uniquely applicable, not universally applicable.

On the other hand, ***if your school's vision of teaching and learning is memorialized in shared agreements and theories of action, the developmental importance of using the quadrant framework is evident. Quadrant 1 becomes and is the target for evolving the performance of teachers and elevating the performance of students. It presumes that high levels of particular knowledge, skills, and efficacy will be evident with high frequency as a means for accomplishing the school's vision and outcomes for students.*** Thus, acting as the Developer, you must ask:

What is your school's Vision for universally improved student results?

What are the measures for having realized that goal?

What is the variety of lesson design and lesson delivery approaches articulated within your school's shared agreements that are associated with accomplishing the goal(s)?

How are they captured within your school's hypotheses and theories of action that, when implemented, will accomplish the goal of improving student results equitably and universally?

How will you supervise, support, develop, and enable your teachers to function routinely in Quadrant 1?

How will you monitor a teacher's progress in using the approaches and in engendering more universally improved student results?

As you observe students' daily learning experience within particular classrooms, what will you look for or assess? What characteristics of student learning and quality of student results will be evident if progress toward the goal is made and ultimately accomplished?

Let us now consider the other two diametrically opposite teacher plots. A "5x5" Quadrant 2 teacher is highly capable of implementing the school's Theory of Action. He or she already has demonstrated both professional knowledge and skill in teaching effectively (i.e., a "5" on the top end of the Highly Knowledgeable Y-axis). However, he or she seldom implements the school's shared agreements embedded within its Theory of Action. (i.e., a "5" on the left end of the limited commitment end of the X-axis). Explanations for those behaviors could include that teacher's passive resistance resulting from a lack of agreement with the school's initial hypotheses and/ or Theory of Action. Because they have demonstrated they can promote student learning already, they feel they don't have to commit to the new school initiatives. Fundamentally, they believe and remain committed to their own self-anointed perspectives on expertise and efficacy.

This Quadrant 2's resulting behaviors may become stealth, noncompliant, or even overtly critical. In any case, their students are both blessed with that teacher's current capabilities and not provided with access to the school's most desired and ambitious learning contexts as laid out in the school's Theory of Action (for example, introduction to and facilitation of academic vocabulary to enable comprehension or learn modeled skills described with that language). By contrast, a "5x4-3-2-or-1" Quadrant 4 teacher is highly committed (a "5" on the right end of the High Action X-axis) to the school's Theory of Action and demonstrates that by attempting to implement the intended lesson design and classroom learning approaches with high regularity (i.e., with greater than 90% frequency). The challenge is that as scaled along the Y-axis, their knowledge, skill, and efficacy is limited. To build upon our earlier illustration, the Quadrant 4's students are not able to benefit from effectively introduced academic vocabulary instruction. Consequently, their independent mediation of challenging texts may be impossible or diminished. Thus, if one describes the Quadrant 2 teacher as "The Resistor," this Quadrant 4 teacher is often "The Wheel Spinner."

Once again, though, I caution you. The same two teachers may perform entirely differently with respect to providing students with Blended Learning experiences. The former Quadrant 2 "Resistor" may actually become a Quadrant 4 "Wheel Spinner" as he or she attempts to shift from being a more didactic "sage on the stage" to a "guide on the side" using and facilitating learning with technology-enhanced and individualized station rotations. By contrast, the former Quadrant 2 "Wheel Spinner" may move easily into Blended Learning due to their prior personal facility with technology tools and their efficacy in mentoring individuals and small groups within the station rotation model. Their limited efficacy when introducing academic vocabulary may have resulted from lesson delivery approaches such as seeking to explain words to whole groups without checking for understanding or by relying upon universally distributed printed definition lists. Again, the point for you as the Developer is how to engage each of these two teachers in both initiatives and move them successfully into Quadrant I. We will discuss more about how to operationalize being the Developer in Chapter Four in which you will evolve from being the Developer to becoming the Collaborator.

Our last dimensions for using the Quadrant Framework for staff analysis are illustrated with four graphically depicted illustrations that follow. Each uses the Frequency Key, the depicted color-coding scheme, and the facilitative questions highlighted in the lower right callout box. As stated earlier, your school's working Theory of Action predicates Quadrant 1 as the desired target toward which you will develop and evolve your teachers' performance and thus elevate the student performance as a result. It presumes that high levels of particular knowledge, skills, and efficacy will be evident with high frequency as a means for accomplishing the school's vision and outcomes for students.

Essential questions will emerge from developing your staff's scatterplot and seeing how they distribute across each of the four quadrants. As the Principal/Developer, the questions provide a roadmap for designing your professional development support and potential supervisory interventions.

How many of your teachers are implementing a particular Theory of Action with BOTH knowledge/skill AND commitment/action? These are your Quadrant 1 teachers.

What proportion is that of your total staff?

In your view, how many Quadrant 1 teachers will be a sufficient critical mass to create a substantial positive shift in your school's student performance?

Are students who do not have Quadrant 1 teachers growing in performance? If not, what support and/or intervention will you provide for their teachers?

Quadrant 1 Graphic

In theory, being identified as a Q1 teacher means that the individual has demonstrated some effective commitment to the school's Theory of Action relative to other Q2, Q3, or Q4 identified staff. However, unless a Q1 is coded in the Orange and Purple zones (a "4 or 5" on both the X and Y axes), they may not actually be your "Top Guns." A "Blue or Green" coded Q1 could be one who is emerging positively with potential both to grow (Y-axis) and expand their implementations (X-axis). Alternatively, they may be only marginally competent staff who are just going through the motions of complying with minimal implementation of the school's Theory of Action as is possible (X-axis @ less than 50%).

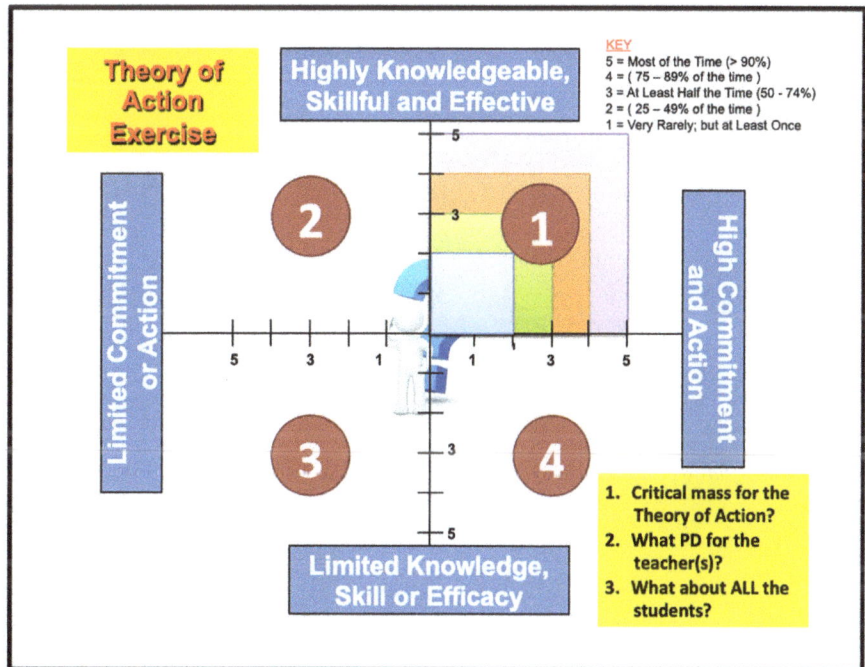

77

Of the Q1s, how many are within the Orange and Purple coded zones? (Generally high knowledge/skill effectiveness with implementation at least 50% of the time or better)

Of the Q1s, how many are within the Green and Blue coded zones? (Generally lower knowledge/skill effectiveness with implementation varying between rarely and less than 50% of the time)

In your view, is a Green and Blue coded Q1 performing sufficiently well when compared with other staff distributed throughout Q2, Q3, or Q4 of the overall matrix? Should a lesser effective Q1's performance also be elevated?

What differentiated support will you provide for the various types of Q1 staff?

When planning your overall professional development program, what priority and with what attention will you provide support for and/or intervention with Q1s?

Are Q1 support and development your starting point, or may it be deferred until you address other Quadrant coded teachers first?

Are there approaches for engaging with Q1 staff and other quadrant identified staff in development at the same time while still being attentive to differentiating your support for all of them?

Quadrant 4 Graphic

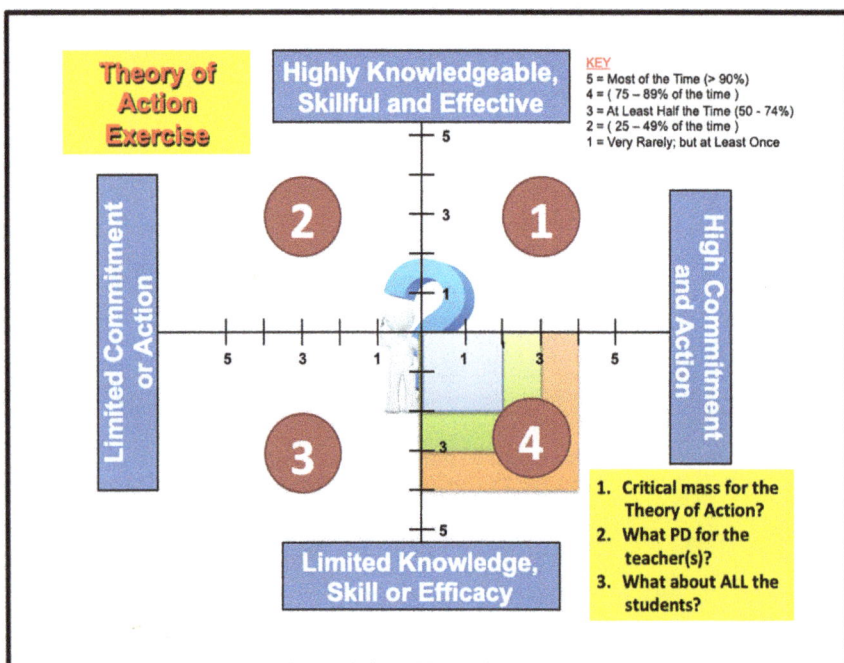

Theory of Action Exercise

Highly Knowledgeable, Skillful and Effective

KEY
5 = Most of the Time (> 90%)
4 = (75 – 89% of the time)
3 = At Least Half the Time (50 - 74%)
2 = (25 – 49% of the time)
1 = Very Rarely; but at Least Once

Limited Commitment or Action

High Commitment and Action

Limited Knowledge, Skill or Efficacy

1. **Critical mass for the Theory of Action?**
2. **What PD for the teacher(s)?**
3. **What about ALL the students?**

A Q4 teacher is investing effort and action in implementing the school's Theory of Action (X-axis), albeit with lesser effectiveness (Y-axis). For you, their more limited frequency and/or more limited knowledge and skill levels pose different development challenges. Any Q4 coded teacher whose plot falls entirely within an all Orange, Green, Blue, or Purple zone needs support either to increase efficacy, increase action, or both. However, though not shown, a teacher with a plotted combination of an "X4 or X5" (Orange or Purple) coupled with a "Y2 or Y1" (Blue) is probably a "Wheel Spinning" staff member with the highest likelihood of seeking and accepting developmental knowledge/skill/efficacy support and ultimately shift into the Quadrant 1 area of the matrix.

Quadrant 2 Graphic:

Just as we have noted in earlier explanations, all Q2 teachers do not function similarly. As depicted, a Green or Blue coded Q2 is neither acting to implement the school's Theory of Action (Y-axis) nor have they demonstrated the inherent knowledge or skills for doing so (X-axis). However, in terms of resistance pat-

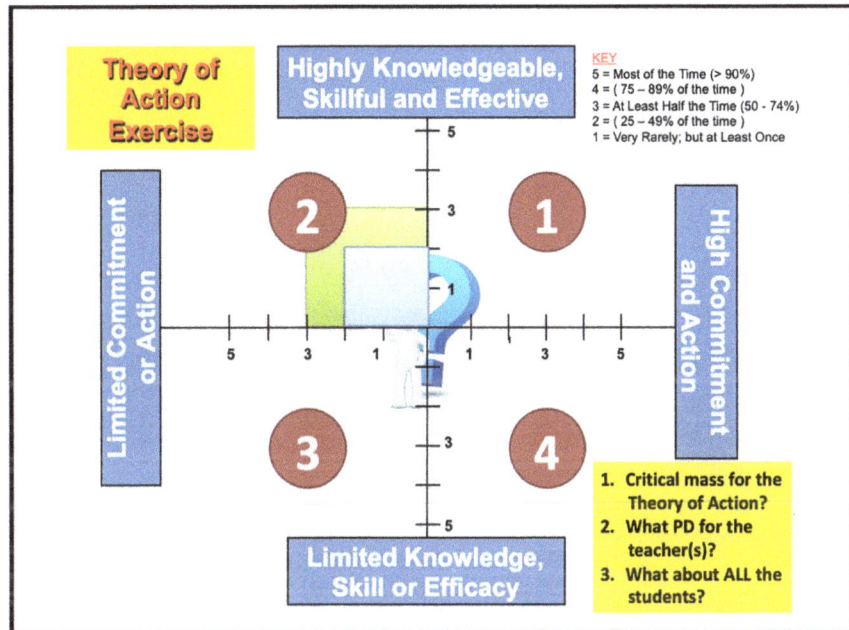

terns and not providing desired services for students, a more serious staff coding (not shown) could be any Q2 with an X-axis plot at a level of 3-5 (virtually no frequency of implementation). If additionally coupled with a Y-axis Level coding of less than 3, their need for development and intervention is more extreme because they are resisting in the context of trying to hide their lesser knowledge and skill capacities. The most unique Q2 may be one we have introduced to you earlier. This individual would be dual coded as a "Y-axis 4 or 5" (high knowledge and skill with previously demonstrated effectiveness using other strategies and accounted by perhaps other measures) along with a minimal level of implementation resistance as an "X-axis 1 or 2." As noted earlier, for whatever reason, this "Resistor" is holding out and will not move into Quadrant 1 even once. You might even say they are relatively excellent but noncompliant teachers.

The questions that arise may include:

Will you choose to leave these Q2 staff alone as "outliers" or "untouchables?"

In the eyes of your other staff, what impact will your doing so have as they witness that person's opportunity to continue doing as they have always done?

Are there ways that you may influence or collaborate with this type of Q2 to engage them more supportively in the school's Theory of Action? Who among the staff might you enlist to help you do so?

What if this particular Q2 is openly critical and engages in influencing others to withhold participation and therein potentially sabotage the Theory of Action implementation? What will you do then?

Are these Q2 types among your lesser priorities or greater priorities for support, development, or intervention as you make your plans as the Principal-Developer?

Quadrant 3 Graphic

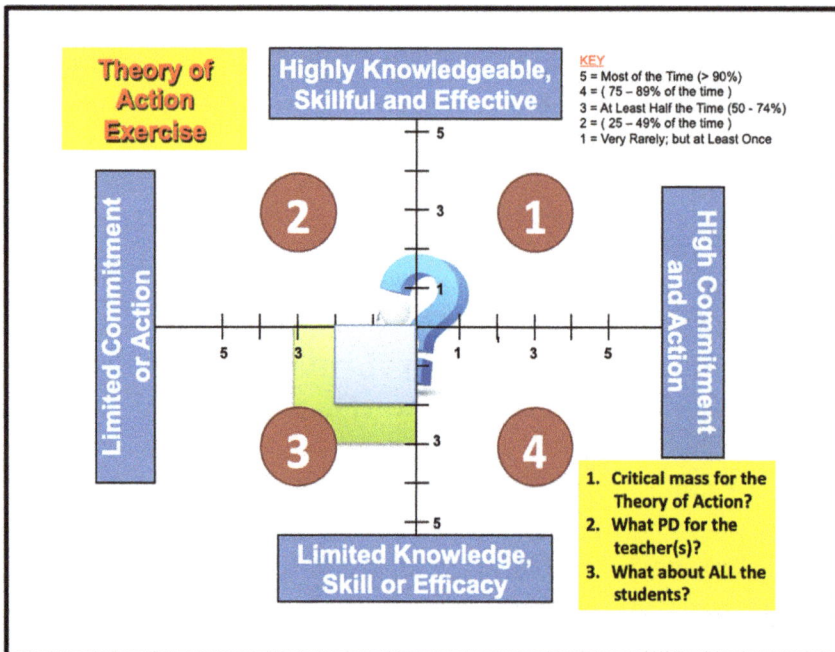

Theory of Action Exercise

Highly Knowledgeable, Skillful and Effective

KEY
5 = Most of the Time (> 90%)
4 = (75 – 89% of the time)
3 = At Least Half the Time (50 - 74%)
2 = (25 – 49% of the time)
1 = Very Rarely; but at Least Once

Limited Commitment or Action

High Commitment and Action

2 1
3 4

Limited Knowledge, Skill or Efficacy

1. Critical mass for the Theory of Action?
2. What PD for the teacher(s)?
3. What about ALL the students?

As introduced earlier, a pan-ultimate Q3 "Dropout" has a code beyond the Green and Blue zones shown. Those are your potentially least knowledgeable and skilled staff regarding undertaking the school's Theory of Action ("Y-axis 4 or 5"), and they are your least participative staff in school initiatives ("X-axis 4 or 5"). At least the Q3 "Green and Blue" zone teachers might be induced to try initiatives even though they might initially struggle (thereby becoming a Q4). Also, they might be provided with the necessary training to move up the Y-axis to

Q2 before committing to actions that would generate future coding in either Q4 or Q1. On the other hand, an extreme coded Q3 (an Orange or Purple) may require intensive supervision if they are more noncompliant (X-axis), and/or more intensive remedial coaching if their competence is in question (Y-axis). In your Developer Role, some of your challenges and issues with Q3s mirror those we introduced about your more extreme Q2s.

Will you choose to leave extreme Q3 staff alone as "outliers" or "untouchables?"

What if this particular Q3 is openly critical and engages in influencing others to withhold participation and therein potentially sabotage the Theory of Action implementation? What if they seek to enroll empathetic collegial support in the face of what they portray as your bullish pressure and their resulting unfair victimization? What will you do then? Can you afford to let even one such person operate unchallenged among your staff?

Are there ways that you may influence or collaborate with this type of Q3 to engage them more supportively in the school's Theory of Action? Who among the staff might you enlist to help you do so?

Are these Q3 types among your lesser or greater priorities for support, development, and intervention as you make your plans as the Principal-Developer?

Quadrant Framework Summary

Your principal's imperative is to elevate the performance of staff and students. You will premise your efforts on developing teachers' capacities to engage students through theories of action that are most likely to develop and improve student performance. Please note the use of the word "theories," for it is likely that you and your staff will generate multiple factors influencing pedagogic lesson design and multiple strategies for lesson delivery and student engagement. The probable reality is that each teacher will vary in his or her initial capability to implement each Theory of Action. They also may be variably disposed to act or to resist commitment to each school theory. Please recall your earlier role as the Surveyor as you now apply your scanning skills to the quadrant matrix plots of your staff. Who among them is improving? Who is declining (or resisting)? And who is adrift like "corks" (simply complying with minimalist commitment and skill)?

Performing a Staff Quadrant Analysis is a means for you to describe a snapshot of your teachers' capabilities and dispositions, but it also illuminates their needs for development, remediation, and supervisory intervention. In the Appendix, I have included a sample quadrant analysis template labeled A7 for your reference. Using quadrant specific questions, you will be able to generate individual professional development and intervention plans, as well as to create a more comprehensive development plan for the school as a whole. You will also find bases for predicting future team learning that can benefit collective shifts toward highly effective and consistently implemented actions aligned with elevating student performance.

Finally, though addressed more deeply in Chapter Four, a completed individual teacher quadrant map detailing levels of capability and implementation frequencies referenced to each of your school's Theories of Action can be a keen resource for undertaking differentiated and developmental conversations in your role as the Collaborator.

The Developer

Endnotes

The Principal as Developer:

- Uses the Vision, Purposes, Hypotheses, and Theories of Action derived from the work of the Preacher and Surveyor Roles as foundations and predicates for development work.
- Engages and participates with staff in team learning.
- Fosters and engages in a spirit of inquiry.
- Expands the universe of professional understanding and practice.
- Develops teachers as designers of appropriate learning experiences within which students construct understanding, acquire and refine new skills, and apply their learning in increasingly more rigorous and complex contexts.
- Introduces and models processes and principles for deliberative staff discourse.
- Facilitates staff inquiry about core pedagogic research to inform both professional practice and student engagement.
- Garners fundamental staff agreements as a basis for principal and staff practice to be developed and held to account.
- Introduces and coalesces a common definition of student engagement.
- Undertakes an intensive analysis of staff capacities for and commitments to implementing the school's Theory of Action.
- Uses the analysis to consider and provide differentiated support and collaborative development that will elevate teacher performance to elevate student performance.

In summary, the Developer Role creates fertile ground for and plants the seeds for staff and student growth. The Collaborator Role will cultivate them and see them come to harvest. As has been true thus far in sequencing this book's chapters and unfolding the first several Principal roles, elevating staff and student performance will require you to work interactively between your roles as Developer and Collaborator. We explore this process in Chapter 4.

CHAPTER FOUR

ROLE FOUR

THE COLLABORATOR

THE COLLABORATOR

As you engage staff in your roles as Preacher, Surveyor, and Developer, you will establish a simultaneous context for acting as the Collaborator. You will create trust and leverage for working individually with staff and for achieving school goals that elevate student performance. On the other hand, to do this, you must distinguish this fourth role from being your staff's evaluator.

Principals have to walk a fine line between engendering staff commitment for change and inducing that change through supervisory direction. The former is more desirable; however, in select and latter cases, you may need to take evaluative action to address individual performance issues. The fact is that as principal, your responsibilities include conducting staff evaluations and your staff knows this. You both may be subject to state-regulated or contractually defined compliance parameters for completing these evaluation tasks, and you could be compelled to utilize specific published rubrics as references for making assessments of professional competence.

At the end of the day, how your staff will participate in these mandatory evaluation processes may be collaboratively positive, or they may submit to and endure them as potentially threatening events. Either way, individual staff could be divided in finding evaluations welcome, relevant, and worthwhile, or nitpicking, loathsome, or a waste of time. To mitigate these disparities, your Collaborator messages and methods for engaging staff must become understood as a constructive process with meaningful opportunities for individually derived value. This will require removing fear from the evaluation process and replacing it with an aurally expressed and permissible language for working together. There is a "secret sauce" for accomplishing this.

Additionally, when participating in shared staff learning and development as the Developer, your parallel use of the Staff Analysis Framework will have brought to light the variable levels of commitment and capability each staff member is demonstrating. Inside of that very analysis, you may discover that substantial staff expertise is evident among pools of colleagues. These capable staff can become one of your best resources for sustaining your principal's work as the Collaborator rather than being kept at arm's length as your staff's evaluator. Through shared staff inquiries, collective strengths, along with their expertise, can be surfaced, recognized for its student impact, and ultimately supplemented and integrated among the staff's practice at large.

The distinguishing work of the Collaborator role is how it replaces a periodic and potentially confrontational staff evaluation process with ongoing

discourse about how individual and collective expertise applies to a common school context of shared purposes. Staff may use their knowledge of hypothesis and Theory of Action formation to guide their deliberations and inquiries: *"What current pedagogy and student engagement routines are particularly effective, that if applied by our faculty more universally, would elevate student performance among more of our students?"* As the staff's current efficacies become more universally revealed and acknowledged, the staff's emotional safety will expand, and its collective inquiry can tolerate calls for new learning. New professional development will less likely be perceived as being arbitrarily or administratively imposed. As Collaborator, you will have created the necessary context to assimilate and accommodate new practices.

Clear the Runway

Whether you are a pilot wanting to land safely with your hundreds of passengers or you are a pilot wishing to take off with a full plane to a new destination, you require a clear flight path into or from an unobstructed runway. Air traffic controllers assist pilots in knowing the landing and takeoff zones are clear and safe. They survey air traffic patterns and assess runways for hazards and ground traffic. They direct actions to clear flying lanes and identify selected runways for only certain planes. Planes circle until cleared for landing, and they line up in sequence until they may take off. Air traffic controllers anticipate and facilitate conditions that permit safe flying.

As principal, you have to become your own air traffic controller or join with other faculty colleagues to perform this function. Even when ostensibly you have garnered a publicly discussed shared agreement to elevate student performance and have formulated its expression in the form of a Theory of Action to accomplish that school-wide goal, your school's runways may be stacked up with staff resistance, inertia, misunderstanding or questionable levels of capacity and competence. When in your role as Developer you apply the Staff Analysis Framework, it may become very apparent that a number of Quadrant 2 and Quadrant 3 staff are neither committed to or sufficiently skilled to undertake specific Theories of Action, nor may they be disposed to monitoring student progress toward desired goals and particular improved results. Furthermore, your status as principal alone holds no guarantee that your staff will get "on board" with you or their other colleagues. Their passive resistance or open defiance might be your substantiating evidence. They may be declaring in so many words or deeds, "No, I'd prefer staying right in my current classroom doing just what I am doing instead of getting on your plane to fly with my students to a destination you're calling our new school."

For you, the point is that you may neither land planes filled with possible means for elevating student performance or take off with your staff to explore and discover new ones. Essentially, your runways could be riddled with personnel produced potholes, any of which may obstruct your school's new ambitions, albeit its pursuit of a moonshot with reasoned hypotheses and Theories of Action to get there. In all likelihood then, you must prepare for and anticipate the need to clear the runways if you want to enable new takeoffs and safe landings with your staff. What can you do?

First, let's state plainly a frequent truth for leaders of complex organizations, including principals of schools. You have no specific vaccine or mass inoculation system with which to suppress opposition, particularly if you are leading toward a bold vision that destabilizes or replaces the status quo. That said, **you can and must take proactive steps to engage staff successfully in explorations and improvements of their practice. It is your principal's imperative to do so. It is also the very essence of your Collaborator role.**

The challenge is that for many staff, your velvet-gloved collaborative outreach may stand in stark contrast to the accountability hammer that they may feel you hold threateningly over their heads as their performance evaluator. If you do not replace this perceived dichotomy early on with a different narrative, it can become a singularly discordant deterrent to collaborative progress toward your school's goals. Staff may seize upon it as their rationale for sluggish commitment to school innovation and their related opposition to change.

Thus, before you confront specific staff resistance or obstruction on your school's metaphorical runways, **start by taking the fear out of staff evaluation and replacing it with the potential for positive purposes and individual value.** You can begin constructing and sharing your principal-staff collaboration narrative as you engage in your roles as Preacher, Surveyor, and Developer. You will unpack language embedded in performance evaluation rubrics (even mandated ones) to support a compelling rationale for collaboration. In doing so, you will cultivate trust, convey essential staff responsibilities for reflective practice and retain appropriate leverage to pursue evaluative accountability as it may become necessary in isolated cases.

What might all this sound like? How might you express your narrative? Based on my experience, this is a two-pronged process with related messaging. Each will rely upon your articulating and sharing particular principles and premises for professional conduct and performance.

1. Establish Constructive Purpose: Quality Assurance and Professional Growth

Let's begin with a foundational point. Teaching is incredibly hard to do. It involves making a set of expertly informed professional decisions and carrying out carefully designed actions. It centers on knowledge of content, knowledge of students, knowledge of pedagogy, access to appropriate educational resources, and the coherent planning of student engagement such that students were enabled to learn and apply content and skills. It also presumes teachers assess the extent of student learning and utilize that data to inform the planning of sequential or related learning experiences. More expansively, then, teaching is dynamic, constantly evolving, situationally specific, and highly responsible for providing students with quality learning experiences. It is incredibly hard to do. For teachers (and other educational staff), having opportunities to reflect upon and enhance the craftsmanship of their teaching supports their professional growth. This suggests strongly that collaboration can raise reliability and consistency in complex performance. Solo flying is good, and there is a lot of that as professional educators. However, having co-pilots to observe and provide us with feedback is better. This perspective understands that the teacher is not passive in the observation and evaluation process. It also understands the so-called supervisor to be a collaborative co-pilot sharing in the common goal of safely conveying sets of students through the experience of learning their way from here to there. If teaching is a complex craft that is incredibly hard to do, then **this kind of collaboration accepts and expects courageous conversations about individual performance to be fundamentally important in raising professional reliability and highly valued results.**

In short, an observation and evaluation process that provides both your proactive support and quality feedback helps teaching. This is based on a shared commitment to quality assurance considered and carried out with proactive preparation, procedures, standards, and methodologies. Planning, protocols, training, and consistency become valued for their service to students. Having reflective dialogue and collecting both observational and performance-based evidence during evaluations is accomplished as collaborative professional work. For example, as part of your Developer role, you will have already introduced the notion of teachers being "Designers of Learning" and utilizing the

Lesson Design Cycle framework for both lesson preparation and reflective practice. As such, each teacher's lesson design process of reflecting upon, refining, and enhancing both the efficacy and the craftsmanship of designed and delivered teaching should already be their daily staff function. Your message can be that during your periodic "co-piloting" with these constructive procedures, purposes, and values already in place, you WILL DO evaluations collaboratively WITH teachers.

By contrast, you can be clear that you WILL NOT evaluate with the intention of searching for what's broken in your staff's teaching. That is quality control work. Its purpose is to inspect and find defects. It seeks to calibrate performance and outcomes relative to standards. It identifies unsatisfactory teaching for its harm to students. It reacts to evidence collected. Its goal is to intervene and correct when expected instructional patterns, student services, and outcomes have been unfulfilled. It is what your most risk-averse and reluctant staff may fear the most. In their view, the quality control process is the accountability hammer principals can wield in evaluations.

However, while we acknowledge that harmful teaching must be addressed as one function of evaluation, that responsibility must be differentiated from collaboration. Generally, sanctioning evaluations that shine a bright light on deficient performance or results should occur based on extreme or adverse evidence and as an exception or process of last resort. You will have preceded them with your many actions to assure that the processes of teaching have your maximum collaborative support and opportunities to achieve success and professional growth. This includes specific support for high-quality lesson design, delivery, and student assessment.

So summarily, here's some possible encapsulating language. In our school, there is no need to fear evaluation or to debate its constructive purpose. We can differentiate and acknowledge a couple of crucial things. First, we always have some growing to do. The nature of professional practice is that we provide consistent quality, and we improve toward even more expert levels of excellence. In our view, quality will evolve with our visions for excellence and impact. Quality assurance becomes our shared process for defining quality and collaborating to accomplish it routinely. Second, unsatisfactory teaching can mean potential harm to students. Therefore, it must and will be addressed. Ultimately, as principal, that is your supervisory responsibility. You anticipate your need to exercise such quality control will be an exception and not a rule of your evaluation process. You will stand for quality assurance and shared professional growth.

2. Establish Shared Responsibility: Unpack the Evaluation Rubrics

So far, your articulated narrative has made a case for a staff's collaborative participation in courageous and honestly frank conversations about their professional performance. You've illustrated the importance of doing so with the imagery of a pilot and the need for reliability and safe passage of students on their learning journeys. You've indicated that feedback and having a co-pilot (i.e., you) increases reliability and improves performance. But what if one or more of your staff members still don't buy into your line about co-pilot collaboration and still prefer to fly solo? Perhaps they feel self-anointed as already excellent practitioners with impressive student results (a possible Quadrant 2 type), or maybe they are more limited in professional skills and have been off the radar screen hiding in their isolated classrooms (a potential Quadrant 3 type). Is there a means you can introduce and use to motivate their collaborative participation?

You must still increase the trust in you and the process. **You support trust-building when you develop and share understandings about what good teaching is.** Trust also comes about when you are transparent and consistent about your purposes and motives. By the time you seek to engage teachers within a collaborative evaluation process, you must be clear that there will be no surprises about what the focus of discussions about performance and results will be, including shared understandings about what professional responsibilities are for optimizing teaching and learning. Without transparency, understanding, and clarity, fear may fill the vacuum left in your supervisory relationships. Fear of the unknown can repress trust. As you illuminate the substantive underpinnings for your intended courageous conversations, the door to trust more fully opens, and participation can begin more routinely.

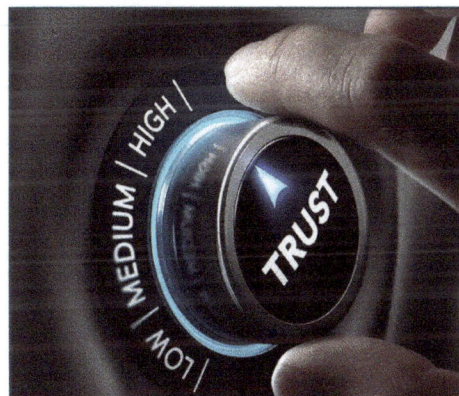

Again, you already will have invested much in accomplishing this. As Preacher, you expressed a purposeful vision for what every student deserved as opportunities and results in your school. You also projected a moonshot premised upon school-wide questing for new means of accomplishing goals yet to be achieved. As Surveyor, you worked with your staff to articulate hypotheses and theories of action, and as Developer, you engaged in garnering shared agreements. You also defined professional practice as occurring within a lesson design cycle of ongoing reflective practice. Each of these foundational elements increases your school's collective prospect of accomplishing ambitious shared goals.

What are my points? You have clarified your purposes and focus in plain sight, and you derived them collaboratively. In theory, and publicly stated in your staff's evolved vernacular and shared language, there really should be no surprises about "what we are working on around here" or "what we are focusing on" when we engage students within our classrooms and educational settings. We illustrated how this could work earlier with examples of schools that chose to design learning experiences that include the teaching of academic vocabulary and the use of blended learning strategies to integrate technology resources across all disciplines.

Yet, despite you having engaged staff in normal trust developing processes, your challenge may still remain to engage your "covert or overt resistors," as well as your "holdouts." These are the staff that most likely will perceive you are doing an evaluation TO them with an intention to change them or even to sanction them. For them, evaluation isn't predicated upon your premise of a collaborative relationship. Rather, it is at the least an "annoyance" or "concerning" and perhaps as dramatic as an unwelcome "gotcha" process. Nevertheless, you can still take proactive steps to replace these negative narratives as they fuel individual staff estrangement.

There is a "secret sauce" within the evaluation recipe with which to do so. **You can mitigate estrangement when you invest time and energy with your staff to "unpack" your school's required performance evaluation rubrics, as well as any applicable contractually defined and government regulated evaluation elements.** The notion of "unpacking" a rubric involves engaging in a search for and a revelation of meaningful language that defines each teacher's responsibility to be both a reflective practitioner and a colleague committed to shared growth and professional development. This goes to the heart of your creating transparency and ensuring there will be no evaluation surprises "on your watch." It can provide leverage for moving reluctant staff toward participating in a collaborative evaluation. Most importantly, it shifts a last remnant argument from the resistance repertoire. You will be demonstrating that you did not invent the *Lesson Design Cycle's* expectation for reflective practice; rather, you derived it from your school's evaluation rubrics that define what good teaching is. Coincidentally and necessarily, you both must and will use it.

Within that reality, the rubric reality, the courageous conversations you will and must have with any teacher, is both permissible and expected. It begins within the construct of reflective practice. It presumes a discussion about the teacher's reflections. Accordingly, the teacher (or staff member) is the conversation starter. He or she provides observations and thoughts based upon evidence drawn from the lesson and regarding the rubrics. You would follow with clarifying questions, additional evidence, and rubric considerations you have made. Any conclusions that emerge, including areas identified for future improvement, would emerge in a shared conversation. This conversation approach supports your stance that you will undertake the teacher evaluation process WITH them. You will not do it to them.

Let us now illustrate how some "unpacked" rubrics describe and define these very processes. My encouragement is that you engage your staff in extracting essential elements for their performance through similar "unpacking" exercises. Rubric excerpts taken from two nationally renowned teaching frameworks will be helpful examples of the potential tabulated results of such exercises. *You may review the table on the next pages using several understandings (see sidebar).*

The excerpted performance indicators are provided in parallel to show how common teaching practices/responsibilities have been addressed across rubrics.

Each rubric provides descriptors of professional performance. The indicator citations for Rubric 1 and 2 are provided using the number and/or letter labels associated with those rubrics.

Each rubric provides performance descriptors ranging from highly effective (or exceeding standards) to not meeting standards (or unsatisfactory). The excerpts cited here are from the highly effective columns of rubric descriptors. These "unpacked" descriptors depict targets for more optimal teacher performance and for having the most desirable elements included in lesson design or delivery.

The selected descriptors illustrate and underscore important source language around which principals may garner shared agreements, as discussed in earlier sections of this book. As stated within the referenced Marshall rubric below: *"These rubrics aim to provide a shared definition of the work teachers do with students and colleagues."*

A comprehensive review of your school's chosen rubric will be necessary. As modeled on the next page, you and your staff can consider how locally defined performance standards and continuums may be used for shared agreements about lesson design and delivery, as well as in professional performance evaluations.

UNPACKING NATIONALLY RENOWNED TEACHING FRAMEWORKS *

Performance Indicator	Source Rubric 1 Descriptor — Charlotte Danielson **	Source Rubric 2 Descriptor — Kim Marshall ***	Discussion — Partial Citations to Consider for Shared Agreements
Planning and Preparation: **Plans for Instruction and the Level of Challenge**	1c - All outcomes represent high-level learning in the discipline. 1e - Plans ... [coordinate] in-depth content knowledge, understanding of different students' needs, and ... resources (including technology), resulting in ... learning activities designed to engage students in high-level cognitive activity.	The Teacher: A.c – Plans almost all units with big ideas, essential questions, knowledge, skill, transfer, and noncognitive goals covering most Bloom levels.	The Teacher Plans: • All outcomes [so as to] represent high-level learning in the discipline • Almost all units with big ideas, essential questions ... transfer • Covering most Bloom levels • Plans ... In-depth content • Learning activities designed to engage students in high-level cognitive activity. Note: The rubrics associate particular words, such as: "plans," "design," and "learning" ... Please recall this book's earlier point that: *Teachers are "Designers of Learning"*
Planning and Preparation: **Knowledge of Students and Differentiating for Learning**	1b - Teacher understands the active nature of student learning and ... systematically acquires knowledge ... about individual students' varied approaches to learning, knowledge and skills, special needs, and interests and cultural heritages. 1c - Outcomes are differentiated in whatever way is needed for individual students.	The Teacher: A.g – Designs highly relevant lessons that will motivate virtually all students and engage them in active learning. A.i – Designs lessons that break down complex tasks and address students' learning needs, styles, and interests.	The Teacher: • Acquires knowledge ... about individual students' ... approaches to learning ... special needs, and interests. • Designs ... relevant lessons that will motivate virtually all students. • Designs lessons that ... address students' learning needs, styles, and interests. • Outcomes are differentiated ... for individual students. Note: The rubrics emphasize lesson plans designed to differentiate learning for individual students. A lesson design agreement could be: To prepare lessons that are relevant, motivational and with differentiated outcomes based on understanding students' individual learning needs, skills, interests and cultural heritage.

* The rubric excerpts cited within this table series have been drawn from a New York State Education Department (NYSED) open-source website (reference provided below). It includes a published list of approved teacher evaluation rubrics from which NYS school districts may select and comply with state regulations requiring that each school professional receive a written annual professional performance review (APPR). These reviews are composed of several components (i.e., classroom observations, student results and other professionally related responsibilities) as articulated with each school system's state approved APPR plan. Each rubric's set of categorical descriptors and component elements often serve as the regulated and required references with which principals and teachers engage in their local school-based discussions about and assessments of individual performance. In turn and ultimately, these become bases for annual APPR documentations.

** 2013 Charlotte Danielson Framework for Teaching Rubric

*** 2014 Kim Marshall Teacher Evaluation Rubric (Revised 1/2/14)

http://usny.nysed.gov/rttt/teachers-leaders/practicerubrics/home.html#ATPR

	Charlotte Danielson	Kim Marshall	
Delivering Instruction: <u>**Communicating with Students**</u>	3a – The teacher's explanation of content is ... through clear scaffolding and connecting with students' interests. Students contribute ... by explaining concepts to their classmates & suggesting strategies that might be used. The ... teacher finds opportunities to extend students' vocabularies ... Students contribute to the correct use of academic vocabulary. 3b – Teacher uses a variety ... of questions or prompts to challenge students cognitively, advance high-level thinking and discourse, and promote metacognition.	The Teacher: C.b –Actively inculcates a "growth" mindset: take risks, learn from mistakes, through effective effort you can and will achieve at high levels. C.d – Hooks virtually all students in units and lessons by activating knowledge, experience, reading, and vocabulary. C.e – Presents material clearly and explicitly, with well-chosen examples and vivid, appropriate language.	The Teacher: • Provides explanation ... through clear scaffolding and connecting with students' interests • Extend[s] students vocabulary • Uses ...questions or prompts to ... advance high-level thinking and discourse and promote metacognition. • Inculcates a growth mindset [defined in the rubric] • Hooks virtually every student ... [means listed in rubric] • Presents material ... explicitly with ... well-chosen examples The Students contribute: • By explaining concepts to classmates and suggesting strategies that might be used • To the correct use of academic vocabulary <u>Note that the rubrics emphasize:</u> (a) teacher scaffolding their content explanations; (b) teacher and student use of academic vocabulary; (c) advancing student thinking; (d) involving all students; and, (e) active student participation. <u>A lesson design agreement could be:</u> To prepare for and organize lesson delivery to accomplish these patterns for routine teacher-student communication.
Delivering Instruction: <u>**Student Engagement**</u>	3b - Students formulate many questions, initiate topics, challenge one another's thinking, and make unsolicited contributions. Students themselves ensure that all voices are heard in the discussion. 3c - Virtually all students are intellectually engaged ... The teacher ... challenges students to explain their thinking. There is evidence of ... student initiation of inquiry and ... the exploration of important content; students may serve as resources for one another.	The Teacher: C.a – Exudes high expectations, urgency, and determination that all students will master the material. C.f – Uses a wide range of well-chosen, effective strategies, questions, materials, technology, and groupings to accelerate student learning. C.g – Gets virtually all students involved in focused activities, actively learning and problem-solving, losing themselves in the work. C.j - Consistently has students summarize and internalize what they learn and apply it to real-life situations and future opportunities.	The Students: • Formulate many questions, initiate topics, challenge one another's thinking, and make unsolicited contributions. • Ensure that all voices are heard in the discussion. • Virtually all ... are intellectually engaged ... initiation of inquiry ... exploration of important content... actively learning and problem-solving. The Teacher: • Challenges students to explain their thinking. • Uses a wide variety of effective strategies, questions, materials, technology, and groupings. • Has students summarize and internalize what they learn and apply it to real-life situations and future opportunities. <u>Note that the rubrics emphasize:</u> (a) the evidentiary elements of active engagement including involving virtually all students; and (b) an expectation that teachers have students explain, summarize and apply their thinking. (c) an expectation that teachers use many strategies and resources <u>A lesson design agreement could be:</u> To prepare for engagement patterns that promote students' highly frequent involvement in promoting collegial

	learning, initiating inquiry, and explaining and applying their individual thinking and learning.	The Teacher's Role as a Lesson Designer and Provider for Learning: • Makes [an] ... accurate assessment of a lesson's effectiveness and the extent to which it achieved its instructional outcomes, • Seeks out feedback on practice from both supervisors and colleagues • Actively seeks out feedback and suggestions ... and uses them to improve performance. • Actively reaches out for new ideas The Teacher's Role and Relationships as a Professional Colleague: • Characterized by mutual support and cooperation • Takes a leadership role in promoting a culture of ... inquiry • Initiates important activities to contribute to the profession. • Actively ... engages ... with colleagues to figure out what works best. Rubric emphases that could guide shared staff agreements: Each staff member will initiate and: (a) Engage in reflective practice to determine lesson efficacy and given cited evidence, will identify future alternatives for probable success. (b) Promote inquiry among and engage with colleagues in planning, sharing, and figuring out what works.	
Professional Responsibilities	4.a – Teacher makes [an] ... accurate assessment of a lesson's effectiveness and the extent to which it achieved its instructional outcomes, citing many specific examples from the lesson ... teacher offers specific alternative actions, complete with the probable success of [each]. 4.d – Teacher's relationships with colleagues are characterized by mutual support and cooperation... Teacher takes a leadership role in promoting a culture of professional inquiry. 4.e – Teacher seeks out ... professional development ...Teacher seeks out feedback on practice from both supervisors and colleagues. Teacher initiates important activities to contribute to the profession.	The Teacher: F.f - Is an important member of teacher teams and committees and frequently volunteers for extra activities. F.g - Frequently contributes ... ideas and expertise ... instills in others a desire to improve student results. F.h - Actively seeks out feedback and suggestions ... and uses them to improve performance. F.i - Meets ... with colleagues to plan units, share ideas, and analyze interim assessments. F.j - Actively reaches out for new ideas and engages ... with colleagues to figure out what works best.	

Unpacked rubrics will substantially focus your conversations with teachers about their performance on both an individual and a collective basis. They are reference sources to describe and define individual professional responsibilities for lesson design and delivery, for ongoing reflective practice, and for collegial inquiry about what works.

The fact that as the Collaborator, you will have engaged with staff in rubric unpacking, further demonstrates your transparency as you conduct your supervisory responsibilities for evaluation. More significantly, it will provide a constructive basis for staff's trust in your being a "co-pilot." It broadens quality assurance to be a collective staff responsibility to fulfill rather than it being exclusively your supervisory responsibility to inspect and document (as would be the case in a quality control environment).

This is the "secret sauce." As the Collaborator, you will create a constructive underlying purpose. ***Your supervisory support within the evaluation process will be offered and provided as a developmental and shared experience.*** You accomplish this by integrating your communication and interactions within your Preacher, Surveyor, and Developer roles with the rubric unpacking experiences of the Collaborator. This imbues those interactions with commonly defined principles and practices. ***Among staff, their subsequently generated fundamental agreements regarding good teaching and professional responsibilities will have a higher likelihood of being valued and collectively applied toward the accomplishment of school goals. Among your potential staff resistors, obstructers, or holdouts, it shifts your possible conversations from what they are resisting and avoiding to how they are demonstrating that for which they are responsible.*** It also leverages those conversations because the rubrics speak for themselves, as do the staff's fundamental agreements. Your conversations are not targeted "at them" because it references and directs your shared conversation toward a joint examination of a set of third points; i.e., the published rubrics and the fundamental agreements.

In the end, **unpacked rubrics** describe and define individual professional responsibilities for lesson design and delivery, for ongoing reflective practice, and for collegial inquiry about what works. In short, you will ***leave each staff member with ongoing expectations for three sets of self-generated professional actions (see sidebar).***

With this clarity in place, ***unpacking rubrics aspires to and pushes professional conduct beyond that which must be enforced through potentially sanction-filled evaluations. It defines the daily work of teachers, and with that, in my view, the choices for what kind of professional each staff member wants to be is shifted to them.*** However, it also slams the door shut on an insidious "gaming" of highly effective professional work. You know what that sounds like as

To be a participant who shares in and contributes to your invited process of developing fundamental staff agreements as underpinnings for school-wide hypotheses; e.g., What student engagement practices if undertaken collectively and consistently will improve student learning and accomplish ambitious results for all our students (our moonshot)?

To be a lesson designer who employs important principles of practice derived from resources like rubrics, knowledge of one's discipline, professional development, and other ongoing collegial inquiries.

To reflect routinely on the efficacy of each lesson's design with respect to intended outcomes and to engage in future lesson refinements to achieve even more effective results with students.

you have probably heard certain disparaging comments made of colleagues. Stories get told of teachers who count on getting by with satisfactory evaluations from year to year by putting on a "good show" during your one, two, or three occasions of showing up as principal to conduct a "formal" evaluation. In their cases, if you were to "drop in" for an "unannounced" observation," perhaps you might then discover a more frequent preponderance toward less satisfactory performance. However, unfortunately in some school systems, the perceived potential for principals acting as evaluative inspectors is so concerning that teacher associations seek to negotiate contracts that limit rather than expand the principal's discretionary "drop-in" visitations and any documentation of collected evidence derived from them. Those staff cultures only serve to tolerate and to protect marginal teaching performance. To be blunt, that does not fulfill bold school visions you are seeking, nor does it satisfy a school's real purpose of empowering and enabling individual learners every day.

Why then did I assert that unpacking rubrics moves professional conduct beyond that which you must enforce through a potentially sanction-filled evaluation? There are two reasons. First, please recall an oft-debated philosopher's question: *If a tree falls in the forest and no one is around to hear it, does it make a sound?* The point of having an unpacked rubric and garnering fundamental agreements is that as principal, you should not have to be there to witness highly effective teaching. By virtue of teachers being designers of learning and reflective practitioners, their daily work should reverberate with highly effective student engagement on a normative basis. You should not have to be in the classroom of every teacher inspecting teaching like a quality control supervisor. You do not have to be in the woods (classrooms) when the trees fall (engagement is occurring) to hear their sound (learning among students).

Second, you will have created an implicit continuum of support options from which staff may choose, and you may engage in developmental supervision. This is perhaps the most important benefit in distinguishing yourself as your staff's Collaborator as differentiated from your being their evaluator. I depict this in the table featured on the next page.

Developmental Supervision *			
A Continuum to Support Courageous Conversations			
The Collaborator			**The Evaluator**
Purposes and Methods			Purposes and Methods:
• To promote self-monitoring Quality Assurance, Consistency, and Reliability • To engage individual staff in dialogue and explorations of their practice • To develop each staff member's capacities for both professional practice and contributing routinely and effectively in their work with colleagues • To provide developmental support along a continuum of options (below), matched in dialogue with the interests and needs of the staff member • To increase the staff's overall scope and depth of highly effective performance ←——————————————————————————————→			• To engage in quality control processes. • To monitor and maintain high standards for professional performance. • To ensure students' learning, as well as their equitable access to and support for achieving valued outcomes.
Goal Setting with Focused Feedback	**Teamwork and Sharing Expertise**	**Specialized Instruction and Referral to Models**	**Inspections of Professional Practice**
The teacher identifies specific elements of lesson design, delivery and/or student engagement as a focus for receiving supervisory feedback. This might include having support for: using particular resources, pedagogy to scaffold student learning, accomplishing a goal for growth and improvement, or implementing newly introduced staff development concepts and strategies.	The teacher requests the supervisor to engage in shared inquiry, problem identification or solution finding about a challenge the staff member feels a need to address. The goal here is for the supervisor to support the teacher with guided inquiry and the generating of options. Together they clarify and consider available resources, possible strategies, and applicable knowledge of content and students.	The supervisor introduces specific professional resources as applicable options for addressing the challenge and lesson focus the teacher has identified. This may include instructional practices and referrals to observe other colleagues who are addressing a similar challenge with efficacy. The goal is to add expert value when the teacher's other sources of feedback and teamwork along the collaboration continuum have not surfaced such options.	The supervisor inspects and measures staff performance using professional standards, student outcome measures and relevant indicators for monitoring growth. The supervisor rectifies adverse or harmful professional conduct. The supervisor takes and sustains corrective actions so as to align future staff outcomes with standards-based assessments of professional performance. As may be needed, necessary protective measures are taken to intervene and restore, or to ensure and protect student well-being and safety.

* This table makes reference to developmental supervision and distinguishing among supervisory support, reflective practice and supervision. These concepts and principles for supervisory practice have drawn inspiration from two works of Carl D. Glickman including: (1) _The Developmental Approach to Supervision_. (ASCD, Journal: EL_198011), and (2) Glickman, C. D., Gordon, S. P., & Ross-Gordon, J. M., _SuperVision and Instructional Leadership: A Developmental Approach_ (10th Edition, Pearson, Saddle Creek, NJ. 2018). Further inspiration to adapt the table's visual continuum are drawn from four mentors whose separate publications and related training have served as my frequent professional touchstones: (1) Laura Lipton and Bruce Wellman, _Learning-focused Supervision - Developing Professional Expertise in Standards-Driven Systems_, (MiraVia, LLC; Charlotte, VT. 2013), and (2) Arthur L. Costa and Robert J. Garmston, _Cognitive Coaching – Developing Self-Directed Leaders and Learners_, (Rowman & Littlefield Publishing Group, Inc. Lanham, MD. 2016).

The context from which staff may elect and engage your support along the Collaborator Continuum is derived from their daily roles and responsibilities. **_Collaboratively unpacked rubrics presume each staff member is a self-mediating (designer of learning) and metacognitive (reflective practitioners) professional._** As principal, you can augment teachers' capacities for doing this. You may collaboratively generate and/or model an abundance of potential questions staff could use consistently to support these daily roles, including:

THE COLLABORATOR

What content and learning standards will serve as the focus of my lesson or unit?

How will I assess student understanding and skills within those standards?

Have I provided scaffolding that has bridged learning from my students' prior knowledge and stretches their learning to new levels? In these regards:

> *What methods or resources am I using?*

> *What would I expect to see if they were working?*

> *What is working and not working as I engage students in learning activities?*

> *Are the student engagement patterns universally true or pertinent to some and not others?*

> *How do I know this? What is my evidence?*

Have I differentiated instruction and engagement to meet variable student needs?

Am I introducing any new student engagement approaches or resources as a result of recent professional development or staff agreements?

Is there evidence to suggest my methods or resources are having an intended impact?

If not, is there something in my implementation that may have affected the results?

What might be looked for to make these determinations?

What constructive feedback would be helpful in my answering any of these questions?

Principals who assume the Collaborator role are investors. You are patient, for you understand that yours will likely be longer rather than short term gains. You bank on the value you and your teachers will derive from unpacking and clarifying rubrics. The beauty of your investor's mindset is in its purposeful and determined use of developmental and collaborative time coupled with your modeling metacognitive reflective practice. **Your return on**

investment will be evidenced in your teachers knowing that questions like those highlighted in the box on the opposite page are shared fertile ground for discussion at any time. And because your investment creates constructive anticipation, you expand the arena for dialogue with them. It no longer needs confinement to periodic formal observations or evaluations. With that outcome, expectations are clear, and trust may grow. You invest so that professional growth thrives, and the craft of teaching may evolve. Imagine for example having many routine and ongoing 2-3 minute "stand-up" staff conversations that explore one or more of your school's fundamental agreements. A quick conversation about differentiated instruction might sound like and include all or some of this brief exchange:

> *"Hi Vicky, how are things going? What are you working on with your students these days? Last chat, I recall you were going to add more differentiated activities in the weeks ahead. You felt that might help the many classified special needs students in your class. Did you follow through on that plan, or did you end up trying something else? What are you noticing? Is there any way I can support you? Perhaps with a drop-in to give you a second pair of eyes? Maybe to have me focus on just a couple of particular things your exploring with certain students? Or would having a planning or reflection conversation be helpful? I am happy to create more time to do the drop-in or talk further. Would you like to set up a chance to do either next week?"*

Vicky's story exemplifies how principals invest in people and yield results. As the Developer, you've already collaborated to set the norms for teachers acting proactively to design and deliver carefully considered lessons. Furthermore, you created a context for shared conversations about instructional practice. As the Collaborator, when you go on to anchor professional responsibilities in jointly unpacked and clarified rubrics, you do not have to be in every classroom every day to "hear the tree fall in the forest." You didn't create the rubrics, nor will you necessarily have to impose them. So, Vicky had already committed to her own Theory of Action for engaging with her special needs students. And without your having seen her teach in weeks, you were able to pick up right where you left off. You were also able to offer new possibilities for shared collaboration. You acted as Vicky's co-pilot, and in checking in with her, you joined in reviewing her instrument panel and how she was setting the controls for the navigation ahead. Also, while Vicky was steering her plane, you utilized collaborative conversation to reinforce your school's school-wide commitment that every student is well-served. And please take note that by engaging intentionally and routinely in those exchanges, you make quality assurance a norm that helps define collective work.

Developmental supervision seeks to reserve evaluative inspections and subsequent interventions for specific individuals who commit egregious unprofessional acts or who risk and bring harm to students. From my perspective, these concerning staff includes those who act outside the scope of your school's unpacked rubrics, and who make the deliberate choice to remain estranged from the school's common purposes and commitments.

This is your second great investment dividend. Your relentless commitment to garnering fundamental agreements promotes a culture of shared development. With your introduction of the Collaborative Continuum, staff may discern your supervisory intentions. In word and deed, you have conveyed that supervision does not need to become adversarial. To the contrary, in your school every staff member has the opportunity and the choice to collaborate on behalf of a common commitment to serving students effectively. Metaphorically, you may now "clear the runway" because your garnered agreements and unpacked rubrics speak for themselves. You will have changed the future landscape for teaching and learning by mitigating your staff's bases for sustained disenchantment, obstruction, and resistance. And in my view, these investments create a stark choice for each of your most ardent critics and your more withering professionals within the 2nd and 3rd quadrants of your Staff Analysis Framework. Self-anointed "besties" or tenure-clad staff who put themselves on personal cruise control may no longer self-isolate or dare you to confront them with expectations. Your conversations among these potential staff resistors, obstructers, or holdouts will shift from what they are opposing and avoiding to how they are demonstrating that for which they are responsible. Thus, stated directly, they must "get with the program and not undermine it," or they will induce evaluation as their choice rather than as your imposition. Based on my experience, the best part of this investment dividend is that ninety-nine percent of the time, you will never have to say this. You can just cloak your conversations in publicly sanctioned language drawn from the agreements you and your staff have created. Generally speaking, I have found that your well-articulated common purposes alone will mitigate potential passive resistance and generate both the motivation and leverage for most staff to participate constructively.

Let's conclude this chapter section by integrating several of this book's now familiar metaphors. Your students and staff deserve to create and engage in shared journeys, flying to new destinations of learning, albeit toward new moonshots. When as a principal you "clear the runaway," you enable new collective takeoffs and safe landings for all. I assure you that all this homework is worth it. When you invest wisely in collectively derived and purposeful agreements, you will improve your potential to elevate both staff and student performance on your watch. In the end, this is your principal's imperative. As you turn these pages, and our conversation continues to deepen, know that I am sharing that imperative as our common vision and purpose.

Share and Distribute Your Leadership Authority

Let me dispel any lingering perception that I am advocating you exercise a principal's supervisory power with monolithic and dominant authority. On the contrary, your fourth role for elevating staff performance is as the Collaborator, not the evaluator. Mine is a call for you to provide differentiated and individual supervisory support based upon fundamental staff agreements about a "moonshot" vision, required student learning standards, and an unpacked set of professional performance rubrics. The previously introduced four-quadrant staff analysis matrix also offers you a resource with which you may identify and assess the extent of variations among your staff as they apply professional knowledge, skill, and commitment to accomplishing common school purposes. *The question we are left to examine here is not how to impose results through dominant supervisory power. Instead, it is how collaboration can develop a highly frequent pattern of Quadrant 1 effective and committed staff performance. The wisdom of experience has taught me that sharing your leadership authority among expert staff is your most pragmatic and influential means to accomplish such a result.*

However, before examining your use of distributed authority in-depth, I acknowledge the extraordinary challenge you already have. As principal, you are expected to lead scores of professionals in a coordinated process of providing universally effective learning and educational services to countless students with a full spectrum of individual needs. Furthermore, your students and their families both deserve and may expect nothing less than your fulfilling this weighty responsibility exceedingly well. I believe we may draw and apply insights about leadership and the direction, preparation, guidance, and process for achieving complex group performance goals from fields other than our own.

http://www.flickr.com/photos/vancouver125/5834658432/
Vancouver Symphony Orchestra with Bramwell Tovey

Consider, for example, the intricacies involved in concert orchestras performing a great masterpiece like Beethoven's Fifth Symphony. You can almost hear it's resounding eight-note opening as you read this composition's title: Dit, Dit, Dit, Daaaa …. Da, Da, Da, Daaaa. All members of an orchestra, including its players and its conductor, refer to and use a common and complexly written set of multi-page musical directions known as the score. It lays out unique performance instructions for each of the orchestra's instrument families and the players within them, such as the strings (e.g., harps, 1st and 2nd violin, viola, cello, and bass), brass (e.g., coronet, trumpet, French horn, trombone, and tuba), woodwinds (e.g., clarinet, oboe, saxophone, bassoon, and flute), percussion (e.g., various kinds of drums, chime, triangle, and xylophone) and occasionally keyboards (e.g., piano and organ). With respect to specific instructions, the score may denote players' relative volume and pacing during particular musical phrases.

Additionally, composers often designate specific performance functions to various clusters of instruments. The string family, for example, is used frequently to introduce and sustain the melody because it has the orchestra's largest number of players. The score may instruct other instrument groups to juxtapose specific dynamic harmonies and accents in relation to the melody. Taken as a whole, a great orchestral score's instructions are generally serialized and intended to integrate sets of synchronously played sounds and tempos from among a potentially full range of orchestral families and their array of instrumental soloists. It provides a guided pathway within which melodic themes and dynamics can develop to create a single coherently played ensemble performance for listeners' appreciation.

Now one might reason that given a score's directive instructions, an instrumentally appropriate set of orchestral players could gather and play a whole musical work like Beethoven's Fifth from start to finish with a simple initial starting count of "1-2-3-begin." In theory, the composer's score tells every player what to play, when to play it, and with what form of musical dynamics (e.g., loudly, softly, and at what tempo). In reality, though, this would be untenable and probably produce a cacophony of unpleasant and poorly integrated sounds. Musical dynamics are interpretative rather than resolute in their direction. How loud is playing loudly? How soft is playing softly? Do these meanings evolve as the orchestra reaches a final crescendo in a later movement of the symphony? Is a trombone's or a tuba's soft going to overpower even the most loudly played clarinet? Will the sheer numeracy of string players' moderately bowed melody overpower the listener's intended hearing of a single oboist's harmonic notes played simultaneously? For any musical phrase, which family of instruments is playing at a fast tempo while another group is playing a methodical sequence of notes at a slower pace? How do the various instrumental families ensure that they will play and conclude specific musical phrases at the same time?

Orchestras play ensemble scores with the interpretive guidance and shared leadership of conductors, concertmasters, and first chair section leaders of musical families. The conductor is responsible for bringing an ensemble presentation to life. As preparation, he or she studies the orchestral score to know what each player and instrument family is responsible for playing, and for understanding how those players and families interact musically, including their relative entries, pauses, and rests. He or she directs this play and interprets the composer's dynamics, musical themes, and counterpoints using a baton, hand gestures, body movements, eye contact, and a combination of signals for counting measures and the beginning or end of play. Overall, conductors create imprints on an orchestra's performance, making no two performances of Beethoven's Fifth quite the same.

The most expert of the first violin family performs several pivotal leadership roles for an orchestra as well. Always seated in the first chair at the conductor's immediate left, this player is known as the concertmaster. He or she is responsible for tuning the whole orchestra at the start of a performance, standing in for the conductor as may be necessary during rehearsals, and for working out and teaching all of the stringed instruments the essential and particular bowing patterns they will use throughout a given piece. For some orchestral players, watching the timing at the top of a concertmaster's bowing can provide even more accurate guidance to progress through the score than following the conductor's unique patterns of gesturing and baton movements. In a similar fashion, each instrument family may have its own expert players, one of whom is designated as its first chair to utilize their skill and knowledge to model instrumental technique and to work out various performance potentials, musicality, and dynamics for their instrumental parts.

There are two points I am making here. First, there is only one maestro, one master teacher, and he or she is the conductor. Yet, there is also an empowered concertmaster and many section leaders who share a maestro's distributed authority. Together, they are conduits for communication and join with the maestro in guiding, coordinating, and raising the performance levels of each instrumental family. Ultimately, though, it is the conductor's unique responsibility and necessary integrative expertise that provides leadership for the whole orchestra, giving its performance clarity, character, and coherence. It will be the maestro's prior study and instructive rehearsals that communicate and "mark up" or notate the score as it is played, stopped, considered, redirected, and played newly. This process coalesces the orchestra's performance to reflect a shared vision for the score's myriad nuances, variables, intentions, coincident effects, and emotional impacts during the piece's many progressions. In the end, an orchestra's final performance is born of a collaborative process accountable to an interpreted, rehearsed, and "marked up" score to which each player and each instrumental section are held accountable by its masterful conductor.

As shared thus far, you may begin to discern several significant parallels and leadership opportunities principals may infer from how conductors distribute leadership and provide both guidance and direction for orchestras. For example:

Both conductors and principals have a primary responsibility to organize and enable groups of professionals to perform a service or set of services for others. Conductors lead ensembles in the creation of a common performance intended to attract, move, and edify an audience. Principals lead teachers in the deliverance of instructional services designed to educate and develop individual students to a high purpose and to serve their parents equitably while doing so. In both cases, being a professional employee is a commitment to serve an audience of others and not the self.

Both conductors and principals must expect that individual professional knowledge, skill, and expertise are shared and not owned. The plain fact is that orchestral players and teachers are inherently embedded within collectives of other professionals who work in parallel and collaboratively to perform frequently interdependent roles responsible for the efficacious accomplishment of results. In the case of players, their collectives are the entire orchestra and the instrumental families of which they are a part within the orchestra. For teachers (and other educators), their collectives are the faculty as a whole and the department or grade level colleagues within those faculties. Conductors and principals introduce this critical expectation for sharing and contributing expertise to collegial development of effective and interdependent performance within ongoing rehearsal and staff meeting processes.

Both conductors and principals also share and clarify collective responsibilities by engaging their players and teachers, respectively, in advance study of specific referent resources. This provides them with essential understandings and emphases with which to perform their individual roles effectively within coordinated efforts to achieve common purposes and outcomes. For conductors, this is a "marked up" score introduced and worked out during rehearsals among instrument families and the orchestra as a whole. For principals, these may include a series of "unpacked" resources introduced and worked out during faculty and staff meeting time. Those can include professional performance rubrics education department learning standards, regulations, and required assessments; locally developed student learning goals; and students' individual education plans.

Both conductors and principals have and retain the ultimate authority and responsibility for their group's performance. However, each may collaborate with and distribute leadership among their respective players or teachers, engaging their expertise in the process of working out and accomplishing common performance expectations in the "marked up" orchestral score, or the "unpacked" and notated educational standards and performance rubrics. Conductors often teach and lead rehearsals with blended support from concertmasters and section leaders. Collaborative principals may borrow from their role as Developer, facilitating staff discussion and inquiry with guides arrayed with focusing questions. They may also model how designated grade level lead teachers or program chairpersons may utilize the principles for deliberation to facilitate and contribute to the "unpacking" and expectations setting process.

Both conductors and principals can expect each player or teacher to have prepared for and to perform the essential elements of their professional roles with requisite competence. This is each professional's fundamental responsibility. To this end, each orchestral player should have prepared, practiced, and arrive ready to perform during rehearsals or concerts with acumen and in accordance with the "marked up" score and the conductor's direction. Similarly, each teacher (including other educational professionals) should have prepared lesson (or educational service) plans that when implemented effectively will fulfill directions and expectations derived from the "unpacked" professional performance rubrics; education department learning standards, regulations and required assessments; locally developed student learning goals; and individual education plans.

Both conductors and principals are in their own ways generalists, even if they remain or have been expert professional players or teachers themselves. They are not experts in the playing of every instrument or the teaching of every subject and skill. Nevertheless, both conductors and principals must be integrative process experts. They act as master teachers of performance expectations and master facilitators for accomplishing ensemble and group goals. They introduce and clarify shared accountabilities, and importantly, they also develop individual and collective expertise with collaboration.

Both conductors and principals must act and must lead with responsibility and advocacy, doing so respectively on behalf of the orchestra's listeners or the school's students and families. In each case, these end users deserve consistently and expertly provided experiences. You may take note that a superbly performed orchestra concert is not accomplished by a gathering of independent contractors interpreting and playing a composer's score at individual will. Neither is a coherently delivered instructional day in the life of a student accomplished as a result of individual teachers interpreting and acting upon performance and learning standards as independently operating educational providers housed in the same building. Rather in each instance, the listener and student experience should be a culmination of carefully guided and rigorously accountable individual and collective performance prepared for and rehearsed collaboratively with their collegial counterparts within the orchestra and the school.

Summarily and said differently, **when conductors and principals share and distribute their leadership authority among players and teachers, opportunities for collegial communication increase.** Common visions or goals for shared results can be explored and clarified, as professional expertise is exchanged or modeled concerning performance responsibilities. Both conductors and principals coalesce this communication and emergent performances with direction, facilitative teaching, and guidance. ***This is essential in their developing collegial understanding of the requisite knowledge and skills to elevate the focused and consistent performance of both individual and interdependent professional roles.***

The Collaborator

Endnotes

The Principal as Collaborator

- Uses and extends ongoing public language to reinforce the school's moonshot vision, common purposes, and shared agreements for serving all students effectively.
- Acknowledges gaps in implementing shared agreements, particularly those that may signal individual staff's disenchantment, opposition, or resistance.
- Creates a trusting climate.
- Mitigates potential staff bases for disenchantment, resistance, or opposition to shared staff agreements by articulating constructive supervisory purposes.
- Presents supervisory support as being a commitment to quality assurance and growth.
- Engages staff expertise in the process of unpacking professional performance rubrics and learning standards to work out commonly applicable performance expectations.
- Clarifies individual and collective responsibilities for lesson design and collegial work.
- Models metacognitive reflective practice.
- Enables courageous professional conversation.
- Provides individual staff with developmental support along a continuum of options.
- Replaces fear of supervisory evaluation with professional responsibility to participate.
- Shares and distributes his or her leadership authority to direct, prepare, and guide the processes used to achieve the school's complex group performance goals.

Your role as a Collaborator is integrative. You make use of incremental elements introduced and created from within each of your three prior principal roles. You add simultaneous value to these by participating in team learning and by guided staff engagement that:

- Promotes individual and collegial achievement of aspirational school results.
- Elucidates staff responsibilities and expectations for highly effective performance.

- Encourages maximum staff participation in accomplishing shared agreements.
- Empowers staff to share expertise that expands professional knowledge and skill.
- Supports individual staff growth, collegial consistency, and collaborative efficacy.
- Distinguishes developmental supervision from being a supervisor who evaluates.
- Seeks to mitigate staff's risk of consequential or negative evaluations.
- Leverages commitment to acting collegially and skillfully to achieve common school purposes as each individual's responsible professional performance choice.

In this and the other preceding chapters, you have explored, assumed, and then simultaneously integrated each of your first four principal roles. I have introduced certain resources with which to engage your staff, to scan and enable a staff analysis of current practices, and then to prepare for and to provide differentiated professional development. These resources included mobilizing questions, discussion and inquiry guides, a quadrant-based staff analysis framework, and a continuum for developmental supervision. In Chapter 5, we will expand your facilitative resource toolkit and examine several additional "tools" in-depth as you act within your fifth important leadership role, the Craftsman.

CHAPTER FIVE

ROLE FIVE

THE CRAFTSMAN

THE CRAFTSMAN

The notion of being a master craftsman is that one is highly skilled and expertly uses tools to plan, design, model, fashion, hone, sculpt, measure, assess, prepare, connect, assemble, construct, and potentially coordinate with an array of other appropriate tradesman to develop that which is being built or created. A craftsman, as intended here, is discernable from other less trained or accomplished workers in that they perform at advanced ability levels and are often responsible for the mentoring, teaching, and supervising of others who are progressing toward and earning specific trade certifications. Within the guild systems of old or current occupational associations, such emergent workers sometimes are referred to as journeymen or apprentices.

Though I have introduced the inherent hierarchy among these designations, let us not lose sight of a critical point. Master craftsmen are teachers and mentors (as in your principal's role of Developer). They also work with other artisans to accomplish shared outcomes (as in your principal's role of Collaborator). Said differently, when you act as the Craftsman, you apply particular tools that enable you to perform your four other principal's roles with skill and expertise.

Considered in this light, principals are master craftsmen. Perhaps your most important expertise is in preparing for and enabling the highest levels of functional efficacy among your staff. Within your previous four roles, you have already explored and experienced using some tools of your craft, including the language of the bully pulpit, moonshot thinking or visioning, mobilizing questions, discussion and inquiry guides, a quadrant based staff analysis framework, and a continuum with which to individualize your developmental supervision. We also examined how your brand of being the Craftsman adds value to collective work by sharing leadership among your staff's expert practitioners. They may become conduits of communication for each instructional discipline and educational service role, bringing to light their unique bodies of knowledge and applied skill sets. Together then, you and your staff engage in guided inquiry, in generating shared agreements, in interactive and collaborative unpacking of professional evaluation rubrics, and in using modeled principles for deliberation to support and enhance collegial capacities for efficacious discourse.

The distinguishing work of the Craftsman role is how you will systematically develop and use particular resources, what I have called tools, as a means for preparing yourself and your staff to perform essential individual and collegial responsibilities. In this chapter, we introduce several additional tools to integrate within your craftsman repertoire. Employed in conjunction with the other tools, your persistent use of these three will prove invaluable for focusing collegial discourse and being prepared to monitor the achievement of collective results.

- The Calendar
- The Interview
- Metrics and Data

Time is on Your Side

As already acknowledged in an earlier chapter, your principal days, weeks, and life may often feel like your time is being squeezed constantly among competing operational requirements. Adding to these demands are the anticipated and unanticipated "incoming" issues that arise from your next email, phone call, teacher conversation, student matter, etc. If you're not on a hamster wheel, certainly you may vacillate between being stressed and feeling overwhelmed. Internally, you may sometimes lament that your plate seems so filled with immediacies, that the critical and important things you aspire to accomplish are not getting done or those you want to pay attention to are not being adequately addressed.

How can the calendar become your ally, rather than a seemingly unrelenting source of frustration or tyranny? In contrast, how can you have time on your side? I have found that school leaders who most productively elevate staff and student results push the pause button on their streaming life. They literally stop their clocks long enough and periodically to create time blocks for intentional reflection and conscious planning. They get off their own daily treadmill and generate hypotheses about how to get ahead of their own curves. They envision moving ambitiously toward an evolved and different future. And critically, as school leaders, they project how and when to engage their staff and school-community in the necessary team building and teamwork activities to realize that future.

Now I know this may sound almost simplistic and somewhat like a mere "Time Management 101" workshop tip. To the contrary, **the Craftsman's process for intentional reflection and proactive planning is far more sophisticated. A school's calendar becomes a vital resource with which to envision, prepare, schedule, integrate, and forecast activities related to desired outcomes.** What does this mean in practice? How does this process work? Most importantly, how can you use the school calendar to effect significant results?

The Calendar Tool – A Planning Timeline

As we have noted in earlier considerations of your four other principal roles, you are fundamentally responsible for guiding your school from its current state to its desired future. The Craftsman's calendar tool will help you to do this. As illustrated below, it employs graphics, diagrams, and flowcharts to depict an annualized timeline structure within which you may prepare for, introduce, and implement virtually any new school improvement initiative. Importantly though, ***it also allows you to schedule these new initiatives in relation to existing projects, staff responsibilities, and school-year deadlines that you must continue to address concurrently. Understanding this juxtaposition of the new with the existing becomes essential as you contemplate the relative feasibility of focusing your staff's attention and channeling their energy toward multiple priorities and responsibilities simultaneously.*** We will simulate these additional considerations within our later discussion of the tool.

In my experience, the Craftsman's calendar tool is an effective school development and project management resource. Its use has contributed to school-wide transformations. It has guided actions that have produced significantly improved student results. The tool's timeline format and discrete elements are adaptable. Over the years and to those ends, I have collaborated with principals and school leaders many times to align its phases and sequencing constructs with the unique focus, needs, and time parameters of their particular school communities, faculties, and staff sub-groups. For you, it will offer means to plan, schedule, and engage your staff and school-community with your goals and results in mind.

That being said, please survey and observe some of the planning timeline's particular visual elements. These include its descriptive text boxes arranged both in vertical columns and horizontal rows, its sets of sequentially arrayed arrows, and its five calendar phases organized with connected sets of descriptive activities. Following the calendar prototype on the next page, extended text will explain its key features in detail and the interrelationships among them.

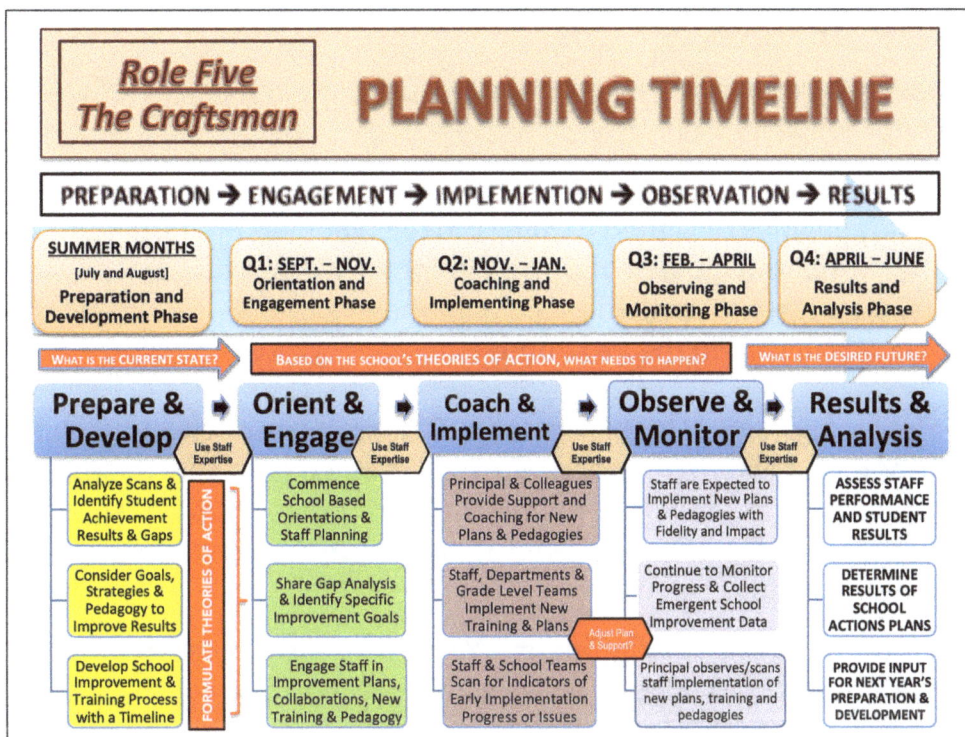

Role Five The Craftsman — PLANNING TIMELINE

PREPARATION → ENGAGEMENT → IMPLEMENTION → OBSERVATION → RESULTS

SUMMER MONTHS [July and August] Preparation and Development Phase	Q1: SEPT. – NOV. Orientation and Engagement Phase	Q2: NOV. – JAN. Coaching and Implementing Phase	Q3: FEB. – APRIL Observing and Monitoring Phase	Q4: APRIL – JUNE Results and Analysis Phase

WHAT IS THE CURRENT STATE? — BASED ON THE SCHOOL'S THEORIES OF ACTION, WHAT NEEDS TO HAPPEN? — WHAT IS THE DESIRED FUTURE?

Prepare & Develop	Orient & Engage	Coach & Implement	Observe & Monitor	Results & Analysis
Analyze Scans & Identify Student Achievement Results & Gaps	Commence School Based Orientations & Staff Planning	Principal & Colleagues Provide Support and Coaching for New Plans & Pedagogies	Staff are Expected to Implement New Plans & Pedagogies with Fidelity and Impact	ASSESS STAFF PERFORMANCE AND STUDENT RESULTS
Consider Goals, Strategies & Pedagogy to Improve Results	Share Gap Analysis & Identify Specific Improvement Goals	Staff, Departments & Grade Level Teams Implement New Training & Plans	Continue to Monitor Progress & Collect Emergent School Improvement Data	DETERMINE RESULTS OF SCHOOL ACTIONS PLANS
Develop School Improvement & Training Process with a Timeline	Engage Staff in Improvement Plans, Collaborations, New Training & Pedagogy	Staff & School Teams Scan for Indicators of Early Implementation Progress or Issues	Principal observes/scans staff implementation of new plans, training and pedagogies	PROVIDE INPUT FOR NEXT YEAR'S PREPARATION & DEVELOPMENT

FORMULATE THEORIES OF ACTION · Use Staff Expertise · Adjust Plan & Support?

Key Planning Timeline features include:

- **A 12-Month Cycle**

Example Shown: July-June

The large horizontal blue arrow simulates a 12-month cycle commencing with the two months that precede any given school year and continues through to the annual end of the academic calendar. In this iteration, the 12-month timeline commences in July and ends in June. You would necessarily adjust your timetable to suit the actual dates of your school's calendar (perhaps June-May). Additionally, should your improvement initiatives require multiple years, the 12-month timeline construct can be applied easily to successive school year cycles.

- **Five Sequential Phases**

Preparation > Engagement > Implementation > Observation > Results

Each new project/initiative will cycle through five sequential phases within a 12-month period, commencing with summer preparation and development and concluding with an analysis of both student and action plan results at year's end.

- **Focus and Purpose**

  Prepare & Develop > Orient & Engage > Coach & Implement > Observe & Monitor > Results & Analysis

  Each of the five phases has a title with its intended focus and purpose. Specific activities designed to fulfill those objectives are outlined in detail with a connected cluster of three distinctly colored call-out boxes. The focus, purpose, and activities of each phase serve as underpinnings for what is addressed in the next phase.

  - <u>Preparation and Development</u> – The prior year's student data and other observational evidence are analyzed to serve as bases for your developing improvement goals and strategies. This phase generally precedes the process of generating hypotheses and formulating theories of action.

  - <u>Orientation and Engagement</u> – You introduce your staff to the year's priorities and theories of action within collaborative activities designed to understand goals, engage in training, and take initial actions.

  - <u>Coaching and Implementing</u> – Staff begins to implement new improvement practices, training, and pedagogy with both your coaching and support and along with that of other colleagues. You and they commence scanning to identify indicators of either early progress or of the need to make mid-course adjustments to the initial project and support plans.

  - <u>Observing and Monitoring</u> – With staff having received and participated in orientations, training, coaching, and support in previous phases, you may now express your expectation that each teacher should be implementing expected principles of practice with fidelity and that there should be evidence of their positive impact on student learning. You will also announce that you will be monitoring teacher and student progress using classroom observations to gather emerging data and evidence arising from staff's implementation. These scans will also provide a basis for you determining individual staff commitment to and efficacy in carrying out the school's shared implementation agreements. That, in turn, will inform your developmental supervision goals for the following school year.

  - <u>Results and Analysis</u> – Within this final phase, you will seek to determine the results of your having engaged with your staff to implement annual improvement initiatives. Together, you will gather and analyze combinations of evidence and data, using it to generate input for the next year's preparation phase and 12-month planning timeline.

- **Theories of Action: From Current State to Desired Future**

   What is the Current State? > Formulate Theories of Action > What Needs to Happen > What is the Desired Future

   These red highlighted calendar elements serve to inform all of the detail within the five sequential phases. They illuminate the continuous pathway of inquiry that inspires and guides each school improvement initiative. They begin with groundwork you laid in your earliest principal roles wherein you discerned the school's current state and then declared the equivalent of a "moonshot" to forecast a desired future. As such, this timeline feature reminds you to premise your planning and scheduling upon the hypotheses you generated to formulate specific theories of action for accomplishing that future. Based on that early evidence collection and inquiry, your theories have predicted that if certain actions take place, certain things are learned, certain principles of practice are adopted, and certain partnership collaborations become routine so that a new future can be realized. Thus, these red graphics are displayed in sequence and parallel with the timeline's five sequential phases. Together they highlight the process of moving your school from its current state to its desired future by considering, formulating, acting upon, and realizing results from your staff's implementing its collective Theory of Action.

- **Quarterly Designated Time Blocks: Concurrent Sets of School Activities**

   Q1: Sept-Nov > Q2: Nov-Jan > Q3: Feb-April > Q4: April-June

   Each phase within the school year is scheduled for a 10-week calendar block and has labels of Q1, Q2, Q3, and Q4. This time distribution corresponds to two clusters of school activities that will be occurring concurrently within the 12-month timeline:

   - Ongoing Instructional Responsibilities –

      Each ten-week set represents a typical school's time period within which teachers provide their sustained Instruction, skill development, and other special and related intervention services to students. It generally concludes with teachers having monitored pupil progress, aggregating assessment information, and awarding each student a summative quarterly performance grade. Frequently these ten-week blocks correlate with student report card periods.

○ Four Phases of the School Improvement Sequence –

The four school-year phases use the same familiar ten-week time structure to conduct each of their explicitly articulated and sequenced sets of improvement activities. **Q1 and Q2 are particularly critical periods of engaging staff in orientations, planning, collaboration, training, coaching, and initial implementation of improvement initiatives. Q3 and Q4 are periods that carry both the aspiration and the expectation that teachers will routinely integrate new initiatives, pedagogies, and training within their daily instructional planning and student engagement.** Weeks 1-20 (Q1 & Q2) occur in addition to teachers' ongoing responsibilities. Weeks 21-40 (Q3 & Q4) are to evolve and transform them.

As represented, these two critical calendar features depict how parallel and often intersecting streams of professional responsibilities must be accomplished concurrently. Principals who act skillfully as Craftsman plan for and anticipate these nexus points. Throughout each year, you focus staff attention and channel their energies such that they may address new priorities emerging within school improvement activities while simultaneously fulfilling their ongoing responsibilities. You use your 12-month timeline's initial Preparation and Development Phase to plan and schedule your school year's opportunities for collaboration and its quarterly training and implementation activities. To do so, you identify and account for teachers' already allocated time for carrying out their daily responsibilities and meeting their many quarterly deadlines. This allows you to evaluate the relative feasibility of your juxtaposing each new initiative's participation requirements within teachers' already demanding instructional schedules. It is also a proactive process and one practical means for you to get ahead of your own pressing school-year accountabilities.

- **Using Staff Expertise**

  Summer Months > Q1: Sept-Nov > Q2: Nov-Jan > Q3: Feb-April > Q4: April-June

You cannot move the proverbial mountain by yourself, nor will you likely earn your staff's trust and productive involvement if you were to impose your planning, scheduling, and activities upon them. Acting as the Craftsman goes beyond merely explaining this visual timeline and announcing to your staff what will occur on a weekly, monthly, or quarterly basis. Quite to the contrary, the Planning Timeline serves as a template tool and is often best completed collectively with your faculty. As Craftsman, your expert skills are in considering how the precious and valuable resource of professional time may be planned, scheduled, and applied effectively to accomplish goals and objectives. So, you may have studied the flow of an annual school calendar in detail, much as an orchestra conductor has studied a symphony score extensively in advance of rehearsal. However, recall that master craftsmen are also mentors and teachers, just as you often must be within your Developer and Collaborator roles. Thus, **with this template tool, principals facilitate staff consideration of time's effective use. You engage them in making contemporaneous observations regarding the pressure points in the annual instructional and assessment calendar. You share and distribute your leadership authority, inviting them to exercise their expertise to garner agreements and to develop and schedule activities deemed necessary for achieving ambitious individual and school-wide results.** This final key element of the Craftsman's Planning Timeline and process is highlighted with four hexagonal call-out boxes positioned transitionally between each of the five sequential timeline phases. As principal and as Craftsman, it remains for you to determine when and how you will engage with staff and use their expertise to accomplish the purposes of your other four roles.

Professional Time – Five Occasions for Engaging Staff Expertise

In actuality, when are these time blocks within which you may engage your staff to conduct the various activities called for in the Craftsman's Planning Timeline? Again, I acknowledge the ongoing march of time and the many responsibilities inherently associated with principals doing their work of leading, and teachers enabling students to learn and grow. In my experience, though, there are at least five ongoing time blocks that can be accessed and utilized to engage staff and their expertise in the activities called for within each of the timeline's five phases.

What is incumbent upon you as the Craftsman is to design, plan, and manage your own schedule such that you will access and use at least these five time blocks to do the work of each of your other four roles throughout the 12-month Planning Timeline.

1. In-service Courses and Curriculum Development Work

   Most school systems and schools allocate financial resources to pay teachers for several forms of additional professional work such as: to lead staff training, to participate in in-service workshops, to revise existing syllabi, and to create new curriculum documents/resources. These are ideal opportunities for recruiting staff teams to join you in planned and scheduled team learning experiences that result in shared development of student outcomes and common principles of practice to guide classroom pedagogy.

2. Master Schedules with Teacher Preparation Time and Team Planning Periods

   This is a perfect Craftsman function; that is, to design your school's master schedule to incorporate weekly teacher preparation time and either daily or weekly team planning periods. Earlier, I called upon you to engage teachers in intentional instructional design and reflective practice. They need the time to do this kind of design planning as well as for reflecting on their lessons' efficacy. They also need routine time to collaborate with other colleagues, whether that occurs in grade level, subject, or educational service-related groups. In those contexts, teachers get to share expertise and provide each other with developmental feedback about implementing new initiatives, pedagogic principles, and practices that work. For you, preparation and planning blocks are opportunities for you to work with teachers along the Developmental Supervision Continuum, customizing your support for lesson design and reflection among both groups and individuals.

3. Faculty Meetings

   Faculty meetings occur at least monthly in most schools. Within these Craftsman planned and scheduled time blocks, you may act in your roles as both the Developer and Collaborator. In fact, faculty meetings can become your forum for team learning and establishing an interactive and professional culture for collegial engagement. Creating this context will involve your engaging your staff in several ways, including:

   a) Introducing and Modeling Practices to Guide Group Work

We have explored some of these earlier. In general, each is designed to increase collegial efficacy as staff seeks to collaborate. Examples include: Using principles for deliberation along with two-phased discourse, employing protocols for providing nonevaluative feedback, and using methods for seeking consensus during staff decision making and problem-solving activities.

b) Providing Coaching

You can facilitate and enhance staff's use of collaborative group practices with real-time coaching and feedback. This will improve their capacities for subsequent usage of those approaches within other collegial meetings.

c) Unpacking Professional Performance Rubrics

This process is one of the essential inquiries you and your staff will undertake. We have discussed how important it is as a precursor to your distinguishing your intended developmental supervision from an unsettling quality control oriented evaluation system. It provides you with the means for staff to join with you in identifying principles of practice that will be emphasized in your school's classrooms and professional collaborations. This transparency is your greatest hope for engendering trust and diminishing resistance to innovation or change founded upon fear of your sanctions.

d) Garnering Fundamental Staff Agreements

This has been a repeated theme within our explorations of your principal roles. It is the basis for your staff's developing hypotheses that will inform their Theories of Action, creating your shared focus and ongoing inquiries for moving the school toward a desired future. It is an essential process for bringing staff attention together to address a potential plethora of different school improvement initiatives. The agreements also ground your expectations for each individual's professional performance on publicly understood principles and practices.

e) Distributing Your Leadership Authority

Faculty meetings provide a safe and noncompetitive environment within which staff expertise may be accessed, acknowledged, and permitted to guide staff engagement, therein coalescing small group input for larger group consideration. Too often, educators' social norms about what is permissible are reductionist, limiting staff and group work to the lowest common denominators of aspiration and expectation. A virtual code of silence is too often enforced to protect lesser performance from the norm of excellent performance and expectations. Thus, your faculty meeting's group work must crack this code and allow colleagues to lead and facilitate each other. Without you creating and validating this possibility, you will have no assurance that faculty will permit or have the collegial capacity and leadership to share in the developmental group efforts needed to accomplish your school's shared vision within other group meetings.

4. Other Functional Group Staff Meetings

Many schools have ongoing functional workgroups with routinely scheduled meetings. Typical examples include sessions when multidisciplinary child study teams draft, monitor, and update individual student intervention plans, or when multi-subject middle and secondary school teams conceive and prepare to implement theme-based interdisciplinary projects. The Craftsman role ensures that such collaborative work is planned and integrated into staff schedules. Without such forums for development and collaboration, such teamwork may not get initiated or accomplished.

5. Staff Observation and Summative Evaluation Interactions

We discussed this key principal responsibility extensively in your role as the Collaborator. You may engage your teachers as their co-pilot committed to shared quality assurance as they out the complex processes of teaching. A classroom observation, then, is not an inspection for quality control. You can utilize its pre and post conferences for developmental work customized individually along the collaboration continuum addressed earlier. This engages teachers in using you as a resource for evolving their practice instead of being a subject of your unilateral judgment.

Strategic Use of Time: Adding Value to Each Principal Role

As you have become acquainted with your *Craftsman* role, your first important realization is that each of your four other principal roles has a time-related aspect to it. That is where the calendar becomes your tool, and that tool becomes your context for systematically supporting outcomes among and with your staff. **The Craftsman simultaneously uses skills and expertise as a scheduler, creating and locking in identified calendar opportunities that enable you to fulfill the purposes of your four other principal roles.** Let me illuminate this all-important Craftsman function within the two comprehensive tables that follow.

THE CRAFTSMAN

TABLE 1	TIME AND PURPOSE – AN OVERVIEW OF THE FIVE PRINCIPAL ROLES			
	The Preacher	**The Surveyor**	**The Developer**	**The Collaborator**
Role Interactions How does the Craftsman Role consider and apply time in support of performing each of the other principal roles?	articulates the vision for a desired and ambitious future. **The Craftsman** ↓ identifies dates for realizing that vision. These dates forecast and frame a working timeline for engaging with others to move from the current state toward the desired future.	observes teaching and learning, collects and analyzes evidence, and generates hypotheses. **The Craftsman** ↑ considers relevant time parameters when creating a schedule for initial and subsequent observational scans.	facilitates discourse, garners agreements, engages in team learning and analyzes staff skills and commitment to implementation. **The Craftsman** ↑ creates timelines and schedules for activities to accomplish each development role purpose (see below).	creates a trusting climate, reduces fear of evaluations and engages staff expertise to unpack rubrics and to identify shared principles of practice **The Craftsman** ↓↑ creates timelines and schedules for activities to accomplish each collaborative role purpose (see below).

Role Purposes
 	
What are the most important purposes performed within each role?
	The Preacher
	Chapter One
	
	• To create and declare a bold vision for a purpose filled destiny; that is your equivalent of a Moonshot. *Example:*
	  o *Inspiring every child to acquire the capacities to pursue a life of possibility*
	• To move your staff to action with mobilizing questions. *Example:*
	  o *What seemed impossible to accomplish before but now must be achieved in the future?*
	• To develop and utilize a shared language to create a Theory of Action to achieve the desired future.
		The Surveyor
		Chapter Two
		
		• To become grounded in your current realities and to project the challenges and work ahead
		• To use high frequency scans to observe student and teacher engagement patterns.
		• To ascertain the quality and trajectory of teaching and learning in your school
		• To form hypotheses about what must be addressed, with whom and by when in order to realize your vision and ambitious goals.
		• To assess readiness and anticipate what is necessary to create it,
			The Developer
			Chapter Three
			
			• To engage staff in guided inquiry about effective pedagogy.
			• To garner staff agreements
			• To engage with staff in shared training and team learning.
			• To hold staff accountable for intentional lesson design and reflective practice.
			• To assess staff capacity for, commitment to and frequency of using intended practices.
			• To prepare a staff analysis to inform your developmental support.
				The Collaborator
				Chapter Four
				
				• To create a trusting professional culture to support individual growth.
				• To reduce or eliminate fear of supervisory evaluation.
				• To share and distribute leadership authority
				• To engage both individual and collective expertise
				• To use the Developmental Supervision Continuum, to provide differentiated support from among its collaborative options.
				• To develop principles of practice agreements derived from an unpacked set of professional performance rubrics.

The Craftsman **Chapter Five**				
• To identify what unique time requirements are associated with and necessary for acting effectively within each Principal Role. • To create scheduled time blocs within which the Principal may prepare for, act and then engage with staff to achieve results.				

126

USING THE CALENDAR AS A TOOL WITHIN THE FIVE PRINCIPAL ROLES

TABLE 2	The Preacher Chapter One	The Surveyor Chapter Two	The Developer Chapter Three	The Collaborator Chapter Four
Cited Persons and Examples of Each Role In Practice	• John F. Kennedy "We choose to go to the moon … that goal will … organize … our [best] energies and skills" • Rhonda Vasquez "Improve all students' literacy levels to 85-90% proficiency." • Kasey Samuels "All entering 9th graders shall be able to read at a … [freshman college] level standard."	• Jack Lowden "There are three kinds of schools (and staff) … Improving, Declining and Corks (those going nowhere) … There will be no corks on our watch … We must establish a shared vision and … cultivate the practices that lead to the results that will be necessary for us to get there."	• Eric Jansen "As your principal, conversations with you will be at the heart of what we do. The future is ours to create." • Peter Thompson "[We] … are going to help our school become an achieving one for all kids … Every idea … [will be invited], explained and considered."	• Co-Pilots "Having co-pilots to observe and provide us with feedback … can raise reliability and consistency in performance." • Orchestra Conductors "When conductors … share and distribute their leadership … among players … opportunities for collegial communication increase."
Time Related Aspects of Each Role	• Articulate a Desired Future distinguishing it from the present by its improved results and/or the realizing of a bold new vision. Examples cited: John F. Kennedy ○ "In this decade" Rhonda Vasquez ○ "Within a three-year period" Kasey Samuels ○ "75% met the new goal in three years"	• Use time blocks to observe current teaching and learning patterns. • Utilize approaches for observational scanning, each of which has unique time requirements and parameters: ○ 30-Day Scan ○ A Day in the Life ○ Context and Closure • No corks "on our watch"	• Be relentless in improving the quality of your school's teaching and learning. • Use time blocks to: ○ Model/use a two-phased discourse process and principles for deliberation ○ Engage staff and community in inquiries, deliberations and decision-making. ○ Monitor progress and implementation	• Use time blocks to model and facilitate the staff's unpacking of professional performance rubrics, and to identify essential learning standards. • Schedule time to explain the Developmental Supervision continuum and to model how collaboration options are distinguished from evaluation.
Planning & Prep Questions Used within Each Role	• Where must our school aspire to get to relative to where we are currently? • Where do we need to be? • In light of these ambitions, what seemed impossible to accomplish before that if we addressed it now with efficacy could enable us to achieve that future? • What is our school's Theory of Action to improve student results that are	• What is the nature of teaching and learning in our classrooms? • What influences that? • What do I need to grasp about my school's readiness to go from our current point A to a visionary future point B? • Who needs to be prepared and/or supported? • What resources are necessary and are they accessible?	• Are there any teaching and learning patterns or common needs that must be addressed? • To what extent are individual teachers aligned and effective in implementing our shared agreements about practice and pedagogy? • What additional support or training is needed? About what? For whom?	• What current pedagogy and practices are particularly effective? • What student engagement practices will improve learning and accomplish ambitious results for students? • Which principles of practice as extracted from our performance rubrics should and will define teachers work with students and colleagues?"

TABLE 2 (Continued)	The Craftsman — Chapter Five			

Using the Calendar As a Tool To Enable and Support Each Principal Role	• Forecasts and schedules target date(s) for achieving your vision for improved results and/or a desired future.
	• Identifies a working timeline within which actions will commence and be undertaken subsequently in pursuit of realizing the vision.
		• Schedules time blocks for observational scans
		• Considers what time factors may influence your hypotheses about when and how new improvement activities must occur, as well as their duration
		• Plans sequenced activities or parallel scheduling
		• Takes into account your school's other concurrent projects and existing school year deadlines.
		• Develops feasible concurrent scheduling.
			• Creates time blocks for staff planning, reflection and development.
			• Takes into account your school's other concurrent projects and existing school year deadlines.
			• Develops feasible concurrent scheduling.
			• Establishes when to monitor the progress and impact of your improvement initiatives; Examples:
			  o Implementing new curricula
			  o Utilizing new training or pedagogies.
				• Schedules pre-lesson time blocks for consideration of lesson goals and how to enable learning
				• Schedules and observes individual teachers.
				• Schedules post observation sessions to engage teachers in reflective practice and alignment conversations while providing individualized support drawn from along the Developmental Supervision Continuum.
				• Uses frequent "stand-up" conversations that engage teachers in ongoing planning and reflection as well as reinforcement of collaborative support

Time is On Your Side – A Summary

The Craftsman's approach to time is to harness it and apply it proactively to your advantage. The Craftsman gives shape to time's use, seeing it as a prerequisite tool for accomplishing results within each of your other four role's specific purposes. Your use of calendar planning and other calendar management tools requires your ongoing attention and action. However, you need not reinvent the wheel. You can transform already existent blocks of time into productive contexts for school improvement initiatives. This seeds the many ongoing daily, weekly, and monthly staff meetings, recognizing them as fertile ground for shared staff development and collaboration to achieve common purposes and bold visions.

In my experience, The Craftsman's time cycle occurs as a 12-15-month process that "bookends" each school year with summer schedules replete with advanced planning, training, and program development followed by an evidence-based analysis of results. In this way, it is recursive and provides a vital springboard to launch and support the next school year's priorities. In closing, your intentional, skillful, and expert use of the Craftsman's calendar tools is vital to your success as a principal. For as it has been explained and illustrated here, your other four roles cannot be performed without it.

Interviewing:

It's More Than Separating the Wheat from the Chaff

The idiomatic expression *"separate the wheat from the chaff"* is centuries old and derives its meaning from typical processes associated with grain farming. Common cereal crops like oats, rice, barley, and wheat are grown as seeds encased within outer husks, also known as chaff. To provide us with the plant-based nutrients and food sources we eat, the harvesting and winnowing process includes separating the valued seeds from within their surrounding husks, and subsequently discarding or burning the chaff. Effectively and regardless of the size of one's harvest, to find kernels of wheat, one must deliberately and intentionally separate the wheat seeds from its chaff. So metaphorically, when one refers to *"separating the wheat from the chaff,"* one distinguishes what is valuable and separates it from lesser things. In the case of considering one's associations with other persons, this might mean you ascertain and choose to work with those of specialized abilities or who are highly congruent with your values as opposed to those who are not so inclined.

As a principal, it may be an easy stretch to apply this expression to your school's personnel process. You may use interviews and reference checking phone calls to differentiate among teacher candidates you are considering for your staff. Certainly, it is a time-honored and routine means for screening and identifying highly qualified candidates and potential new employees, while separating them from others who are less a match for your requirements. However, I submit that interviews can become so much more valuable than a winnowing process that separates the wheat from the chaff. It is a vital tool that supports each of your roles as the Preacher, the Surveyor, the Developer, and the Collaborator. Acting as the Craftsman, you will do this by designing each series of school interviews based upon some very strategic engagement with your staff.

It begins with this reality. Consider that your interviews are a two-way recruitment process. As the school, you want to attract interested and capable candidates who fulfill your staff or position profile. Consider, though, that in your demeanor, setting, questions, and level of interactive engagement, you are also communicating who you are as a school and the kind of professional associate or supervisor you may be for the candidate. ***Thus, interviews are not just your selection process. Your candidates may be selecting you as well.*** Who are you and your staff being when you conduct an interview? Would you want to work for you? Would you want to commit your professional life to a school that stood for what you stand for? Have you even conveyed what you stand for and what it will be like to participate in the professional life of your school?

Engaging with your staff to design an interview process is an opportunity to accomplish several important things:

Coalesce staff agreements in advance about:

What the school's current goals are (e.g., 85-90% reading proficiency)

What the school's future needs are (e.g., To hire more dual certified staff who can increase student literacy and support within inclusive classrooms)

What is valued in classroom instruction and among your educational services

What teacher qualities may fulfill those needs and share those values

Develop interview questions that simulate real tasks and responsibilities to assess a candidate's potential for quality performance and valued contributions;

Develop an interview approach that allows you to introduce and convey:

What is important about the school (e.g., interdisciplinary teams, career planning, electives that include the arts/music and co-curricular activities).

What is valued by the school (e.g., home-school communication).

What is valued in classroom instruction (e.g., rigorous learning, inquiry, early literacy, and using technology as an integrated tool for learning).

What is valued in educational services (e.g., social-emotional learning).

What are the expected and desired working relationships among one's colleagues (e.g., active participation in faculty meetings, team planning periods, and staff-training sessions).

I am advocating that within your interviews, candidates have the experience of being a potential staff member and colleague. Later in this section, we will explore more about how engaging your staff as the Craftsman will help you to create and use the interview as a tool associated with the purposes of your other roles. For now, let me illustrate some questions as I have heard them posed within a single interview. These have invited candidates to interact with you in just the manner I have been introducing.

Illustration 1

"Welcome, Miss Bambridge. We are pleased to have you join us today. Here at Mill River School, we believe in three core principles: having strong literacy skills enables early and sustained abilities to engage in challenging learning; each student's social-emotional learning is as important as developing his or her cognitive abilities and communication skills; and finally, a complete education includes participation in the arts and other extracurricular opportunities.

- As a new member of our staff, please describe for us how your classroom and your participation in our school will support these three principles?

- Please also feel welcome to share other principles you believe are important to incorporate in your students' learning experiences."

Illustration 2

"Miss Bambridge, as you know, in our state, it is possible to earn tenure as a certified teacher following three successful years in your teaching assignments. Let's imagine for a moment that we can fast-forward together into our future three years from now. Imagine further that we are sitting down and having our tenure evaluation conference. We recall in that conference how today in this first candidate interview, we let you know that there would always be two bottom-line essential things in your performance here at Mill River School. First, your students are better off because you are their teacher. Second, that this faculty is better off because you are a member of it.

With these points in mind, here are the questions, and if you wish, please ask us to repeat them. In that future tenure evaluation conference three years from now, what will you be able to say and celebrate about each of those two important bottom line things?

- First, who will you have been as your students' teacher, and what will you have accomplished?

- Second, why will our faculty and this staff be better off because you have been our colleague?

- Please also know that while today is a simulation, we really will have this conversation in three years. Take your time, and then please share your thoughts and answers."

Illustration 3

"Thank you again, Miss Bambridge, for our time together. We will now conclude our interview with one final set of questions. Once again, if you wish, please feel welcome to ask us to repeat them before you answer. Based on our interview team's questions of you today and perhaps what you may already know about Mill River School, what do you think about each of these three related questions:

- What is important at Mill Road School?

- What kind of professionals do we seek as members of our staff?

- Why are you interested in joining us?"

At this juncture, it may strike you that candidate interviews, along with their associated staff preparations and debriefings, are just additional examples of allocated blocks of time. You may feel we already addressed this aspect of your fifth role in our last section. You recall that the Craftsman creates integrated schedules that anticipate school deadlines and earmark interactive time to perform the functions of your other four principal roles. This is the process, while the resulting calendars and timelines are the Craftsman's tools.

Nonetheless, an interview is more than a vital block of time that you anticipate and schedule proactively. It is a fundamental rethinking of traditional recruitment and screening outcomes. You become more than a skilled and expert scheduler, and your results are more than a candidate's selection. **You utilize candidate interviews as your incubator, creating a context for intentional staff and candidate interactions.** You design these interactions with two results in mind:

Continuity and Development

Before candidates have even walked in the interview door, you renew and coalesce your staff's clarity about what they stand for as educators, what they are doing, why that is important, how they work together, and by when they intend to achieve their goals. This ensures that you base the interview's design upon a collective commitment to the continuous development of both your fledgling and robust school improvement initiatives. It also ensures that any emergent challenges are at least identified and considered for future development.

Orientation and Onboarding

Your interview also commences your school's onboarding process. You and your staff will use it as an initial introduction to your professional community. You will design its questions and simulated real-world scenarios to orient and inspire potential new colleagues. Your interview seeks not only to have the candidate accept an offer of employment but also to invest in accomplishing your school's purposes with a commitment to its principles and practices.

In my experience, **the results of a well-crafted interview are that you will have jumpstarted future colleagueship.** You will have reinforced and deepened your staff's norms for collaboration by engaging them in the design of the interview. Finally, its questions help new candidates learn what your school values are and how to be a part of its professional teamwork.

Within this expanded view of your Craftsman role, you are a designer of collegial learning and professional engagement. Your interviews are controlled growth contexts for present and future staff's interactions, engendering both collective focus and shared capacities for sustainable development and collaboration. Your tools are reflective discourse, thought-provoking questions, and contextualized professional simulations. Your materials are your school's values and norms fashioned with crafted language derived from the stance of each principal role.

Let me illustrate some source material the Craftsman may design with:

From The Preacher:

- What is the future we are pursuing for our school and our students?
- By when are we striving to be there?

From The Surveyor:

- What is going on around here?
- What is the nature of teaching and learning in our classrooms?
- What hypotheses have we formulated about how to pursue our future goals?

From The Developer:

- How do we learn and grow together?
- How do we engage effectively during inquiry, discourse, and deliberations?
- What are the things we are committed to being skillful about?

From The Collaborator

- What are our valued principles of practice?
- How is leadership shared and staff expertise acknowledged in our school?
- How is accountability expected while ensuring that there are trust and support?

Interviewing – A Summary

When you design interviews as the Craftsman, you do three things. First, you reinforce your school's goals, values, and accomplishments among your existing staff by involving them in the process of crafting the interview's questions. Second, you create and simulate your school's context for the candidates who will ultimately become your new colleagues. Third, you also model how you value and share your leadership by engaging your staff's expertise in the design process. To recap and reinforce once again, the Craftsman's design tools integrate the purposes to be fulfilled by acting in your four other roles.

Metrics and Data are Your Friends

Acknowledging that there are whole volumes that deeply consider this subject, your most basic principal toolkit would be incomplete without substantial attention to the Craftsman's skilled process of metric-based visioning and of expert use of data-informed analysis. These are crucial in your being able to elevate student and staff performance. During my fortunate experience of leading countless schools, I have used student performance data to coach teachers and to empower our data teams to generate school improvement action plans. In every instance, metrics and data were not a source of fear. Rather, they were employed to guide our reflective practice as lesson designers and to provide means for our benchmarking and tracking progress toward specific goals. Hence in this section, I will offer insight into how as the Craftsman, you will design a metrics-based and data-informed metacognitive process for your staffs' use. We begin as we have before with scenarios to illustrate aspects of this exploration.

Scenario 1

One day while doing a home project, my Dad passed along an old adage as he was teaching me how to use his woodworking tools. "Measure twice and cut once." Using a scrap of wood, he demonstrated how to double-check my measurement's accuracy before cutting into the lumber lest I mistakenly render the resulting two pieces useless and the original lumber wasted. He cautioned that this would only increase my project's expense and my need for additional time to complete it. However, what really stuck with me was the advice he served up next. To this day, I apply it still. With his ruler and saw in hand, he looked me in the eyes and said, "Son, what we are doing now actually applies to your life. Plan and prepare carefully and methodically before taking action. You cannot afford to waste what you have or waste another person's time. Besides, you may earn those things or have their attention only once."

Scenario 2

Competitive athletes and performing artists often share at least one common experience. In trying out for a team or in auditioning for a place within an ensemble cast, dance troupe, or orchestra, they inevitably must confront questions like: "Did I make the cut? Was I good enough to continue to the next round? Did I make the team or ensemble or not?" The plain truth is that in life, our performance is measured and assessed frequently. To move forward, we either exceed what is necessary to qualify, or we demonstrate what is defined as excellent. Life's criteria and metrics are often defined for us in advance, and so too are its benchmarks. So rarely are we selected just because we happen to be the best of the bunch that tried out. To the contrary, performing well will always be important, but making the cut is something quite different.

As a school principal, I suspect that you will grapple with the issues these scenarios raise many times over. Both you and your staff regularly conduct assessments. If your assessment systems are sophisticated, you probably employ multiple measures and have established a scaled matrix that aggregates or integrates the various performance indicators. In effect, when appraising individual student and teacher performance, your school may "measure twice before cutting once" along your local version of a benchmarked criterion line. However, for the assessed individual, preparing and striving to do well, or even doing one's personal best in these situations may be insufficient to exceed the essential benchmarks. Performing well will be significant and consistently encouraged but knowing and being able to do what is acceptable or sufficiently excellent may be what is ultimately necessary.

In the end, your criterion-based benchmarks can function as blunt instruments. Measurements may happen many times, but the cut often comes only once. Students either pass an exam, or they don't. They either earn credit for a course, or they don't. As individuals, a student will either have the qualifying score(s) for selection to an advanced class or to earn a college scholarship, or that student will not. In fact, a student with depressed performance scores may become identified to receive remedial or other special educational services.

Among teachers, their annual evaluations may have a similarly consequential impact. For example, perhaps your school or system offers annual performance pay awards based upon multiple measures with an evaluation score drawn from a matrix of rubrics and other criteria. Let's suppose that "making the cut" in this instance required a teacher to earn a benchmark rating of "highly effective" as a precondition for having an incentive award added to their ensuing year's base salary. All the other teachers would have received performance ratings distributed along a hypothetical scaled continuum ranging from "effective" to "developing" to "ineffective." However, further applying the same scoring matrix, let's imagine that there was also a minimum "cut line." For those who might have earned a "developing" or an "ineffective" rating, they would need to implement a subsequent performance

137

improvement plan with administrative oversight. Clearly, in that school or that system, the evaluation model implicitly conveys an expectation that every teacher must perform at least "effectively." The consequence of not meeting expectations, of teachers not "making the cut," would yield highly contrasting results. The "cut line" functioned as a demarcation threshold. Either the teacher would earn access to significantly positive salary incentives, or they would become subject to evaluative interventions.

The point is that your students' and teachers' lives are at stake. As principal, you cannot allow their futures to be compromised with ill-planned assessments, ill-conceived criteria, ill-founded benchmarks, or inaccurately implemented evaluation systems. While I acknowledge that state regulations, district policies, or contractually negotiated agreements may impose directives and limit your school's freedom to act independently, you and your staff must heed the implications of *Scenario 1's* cautionary call. You can ill afford to waste valuable resources, especially your students' and staff's invested time and their respective personal pathways to desired outcomes.

That said, wasting time is just not in the Craftsman's mindset. You will recall from the earlier discussion that the Craftsman gives shape to time's use, seeing it as a prerequisite resource for accomplishing results within each of your other four role's specific purposes. Yet, harnessing and applying time within masterfully designed schedules is a different skillset from measuring accurately to reveal current performance levels, or scaling measurements relative to desired performance standards. In the world of educational performance assessment, measuring with accuracy to yield information of value is different from providing an efficient testing schedule or scoring system. So, if while acting as the Craftsman, contributing to time's productive use is highly valued, what is at issue here is not the waste of time per se, but the potential value of the yield derived from the measurement tools themselves.

Stated plainly, master craftsmen know tools, including how to select and use each with skill and accuracy. They know how to apply tools creatively and appropriately in sequences or in combinations to affect desired results. Frequently, those results are established with design specifications necessitating accurate measurement and integration of coordinated tasks. Taken together, master craftsmen are results-oriented. In your school setting, the Craftsman's tools are assessment and evaluation instruments, data and evidence collection systems, and an array of associated measurement scales, rubrics, and matrices. In and of themselves, the data and the evidence derived from using the measurement and collection tools are neutral. It is just information. On the other hand, the designated scales, rubrics, and matrices give meaning to the data and evidence. They are critical interpretive tools with which to inform your subsequent developmental and collaborative considerations with staff.

My recommendation here is direct. Push the pause button on your current stream of existing assessment practices. Stop and take a reality check as it relates to your school's measuring student and staff performance or as you may be applying summative criteria and benchmarks deterministically. Consider deeply the impact or limitations of what you are doing. I am calling upon every principal to act proactively within the scope of your discretion. I am also calling upon you to supplement existing assessments with additional instruments as may be beneficial to crafting more overall informed evaluations.

Within this stance as the Craftsman, consider yourself to be a catalyst for accomplishing collective results through your other four principal roles. In particular, as Preacher and Developer, you will have articulated an ambitious vision and created or garnered shared staff agreements for school outcomes. You will stimulate an ongoing need for collective staff inquiry, such as, "How will we know if we are progressing toward and achieving our goals?"

As Surveyor, you may seed those inquiries with some "snapshots" drawn from your recent scans of student performance data and observational evidence of current teaching and learning patterns within the school. As Developer and Collaborator, you will engage with your staff in team learning and encourage their sharing of expertise about how to make productive use of student and staff assessment tools. You can also stimulate their shared reflection about whether your current tools are appropriate and meaningful measures to calibrate performance, establish benchmark criteria, and ultimately make data-informed "cuts." ***Thus as Craftsman, when you catalyze all these vital processes with transparent access to information about the nature of student and staff assessment tools and the data that arises from them, you act proactively to diminish fear and eliminate potential staff resistance to data-informed progress monitoring and shared responsibility for collective results.***

As principal, you operationalize these processes by asking simply:

- The Craftsman
  - What are my current tools, and what other tools may be potentially useful?
  - Specifically, what assessment and evaluation instruments, data and evidence collection systems, and associated measurement scales, rubrics, and matrices are in use? Or have not been introduced?
  - Which tools align with accomplishing the intended outcomes of my other four principal roles?
  - What skills are required and understood regarding each of their use?
  - How can I model and teach the use of multiple measures to better inform the professional actions I may take, or my teachers may take?
- The Preacher –
  - What are our school's goals and vision for student and staff performance?
  - For what purpose(s) are data and other evidence being collected and subsequently used?
- The Surveyor –
  - Based on what we know about what's going on in

THE CRAFTSMAN IN ACTION
<u>TWO CASE STUDIES REVISITED</u>

In Chapter One, you were introduced to school administrators Rhonda Vasquez and Kasey Samuels. Each used their Preacher's bully pulpit to declare a literacy defined "moonshot." In both cases, new performance- based reading goals were set based on their initial Surveyor scans of current student performance levels. For Rhonda, 3 out of 4 schools performed below state reading proficiency levels, with one's 53% student proficiency score being among the lowest of 13 neighboring school systems. For Kasey, initial data revealed that only 33% of entering 9th graders could demonstrate independent abilities to comprehend 90% of texts if written at a graduation standard level of difficulty.

Both these leaders were substantially expert in understanding how to measure and monitor individual pupil progress in developing the independent capacities to read. They also possessed the expert knowledge and skills for how to scale those pupil results meaningfully to inventories correlated with real world functional text difficulty. They were acting as a Craftsman whose expertise informed their moonshots (what was desirable as future school outcomes) and also provided lenses with which to scan current data and to observe classroom patterns skillfully.

Both Rhonda and Stacey would go on to use their Craftsman knowledge and skills to catalyze intensive rounds of staff discussion and professional development in their roles as Developer and Collaborator. New means for improving student results were introduced, including: (1) To empower school reading specialists as internal coaches who would collaborate with teaching colleagues to assess text difficulty prior to text use and to design lessons that enabled students to mediate increasingly difficult texts; (2) To monitor ongoing individual student growth in decoding and in reading comprehension using text based reading inventories; and, (3) To supplement state testing with locally administered reading assessments that provided both diagnostic data and comprehension data correlated to text difficulty and independent reading levels.

our school, what is our working theory about what we will require to accomplish our future goals and vision for students and staff?

- What value is being provided by our current assessments and the data we are deriving from them? And what value are we getting from the other evidence we are observing or collecting?
- Is this data, and are these collections of evidence aligned with our theory of what information we will require to achieve our goals and vision for students and staff?
- Do our performance measures define what students and teachers must know and be able to do?
- Do we define our cut scores and benchmarks concomitantly? Do they define more than minimum acceptable performance? Do they also define level(s) of excellence consistent with the highest aspirations for our school's goals and vision?

- The Developer
  - If we use our measurement tools as designed, do they inform and guide our progress toward our desired outcomes?
  - Are we using our measurement tools with the intended accuracy, skill, and consistency to be equitable to all persons undergoing evaluation?

- The Collaborator –
  - Does the data illuminate what is important, albeit what may be utilized to make a positive difference in the quality of teaching and the scope of learning in our school?
  - Are there performance measures that should be added or eliminated to get increased value from our entire assessment system?

Metrics and Data are Your Friends – A Summary

The metrics and data derived from appropriately designed or selected assessment tools may be used to support your school's collective efforts to achieve shared goals. Acting as the Craftsman, principals are critical catalysts in that process. Together, you can hold your progress measures accountable to the high purpose of informing improvements in teaching and learning. You do this as you collaborate with staff in examining current assessment practices and analyzing their data. You use these reviews to inform necessary professional development and to guide actions toward a shared future vision. In doing so, you will have made a remarkably significant contribution to your school's capacities for realizing educational growth, tracking improvement, and achieving desired results.

The Craftsman
Endnotes

The Principal as Craftsman

- Uses a variety of tools with skilled expertise to inform and support performance within each of the other four principal roles.
- Plans, designs, and provides resources to guide and facilitate outcomes associated with performing the other four principal roles.
- Models the use of specific tools or engages with expert staff practitioners to add value to their applications.
- Creates incubators for development and collaborative work.

Examples of the Craftsman's Tools and Resources at Work:

- Crafting visionary language
  - Used to inspire others with aspirational goals, and to forecast new potential futures with "moonshot" thinking.
- Crafting mobilizing questions
  - Used to assess one's current state so as to invite staff to inquire and call them to action in pursuit of achieving essential school purposes.
- Crafting discussion and inquiry guides
  - Used to support deliberation and discourse.
- Crafting a quadrant-based staff analysis framework
  - Used to consider and assess staff skills and commitment with respect to being aligned with and implementing shared agreements and new strategies.
  - Used to differentiate and plan developmental supports and interventions.
- Crafting a continuum of developmental supervision
  - Used to distinguish one's collaborator role from that of being an evaluator.
  - Used to engage staff in courageous conversations, engender reflective practice and enable support to be elected from among a continuum of options.
- Crafting a 15-month Planning Timeline
  - Used to develop master schedules and requisite time blocks associated with the ongoing school need for functional, developmental, and collaborative time.
  - Used to guide school improvement initiatives through a planned and multi-phased cycle of implementation and evaluation.

- ○ Used to integrate and coordinate a school's many ongoing activities and deadlines with its annual improvement initiatives.
- Crafting Interviews
    - ○ Used to design a collegial learning and professional engagement process.
    - ○ Used to reinforce school goals, values, and accomplishments among staff.
    - ○ Used to create and simulate a school context for employee candidates.
    - ○ Used to engage staff expertise and to share leadership in the design process.
- Using Assessment Tools and Performance Measures
    - ○ To identify and use relevant metrics and data derived from assessment tools selected because they measure desired levels of performance and monitor individual progress toward essential learning outcomes.
    - ○ To engage staff in the continuous improvement of the tools used to assess teaching and learning and support the achievement of valued school results.

CHAPTER SIX

WHERE WILL YOU BEGIN?

Where will you begin? On your watch, how will you elevate your school's performance? How might you enhance the efforts already underway? I trust that I have been clear what experience has taught me. It is in having both an inspiring shared purpose and in augmenting your school's capacities for effective teaching and learning. My espoused Theory of Action premises that if your leadership focuses upon and develops your staff's knowledge and skills about effective teaching, then their coming to a shared agreement regarding collective school practices is possible. This, in turn, will result in improved student learning and be measured in positive trajectories for student performance results.

You have a menu of five synergistic roles with which to do this work. What will you aspire to, and how will you mobilize your school (The Preacher role)? How will you call your staff to the high purpose and inject focal energy? What evidence will you draw from your early scans (The Surveyor role) or from your observations of current and evolving classroom practices? How will this evidence inform your emergent hypotheses and related theories of action? To breathe life into those theories, how can you utilize team learning (The Developer role)? What will you and your staff clarify as the essential knowledge and effective skills for engagement — of each other in deliberative discourse, as well as of students in classroom learning or educational services? How will you provide differentiated staff support and distribute your leadership authority among staff experts (The Collaborator role) to accomplish excellence in shared performance? Finally, from among an array of expert skills to prepare, design, schedule, and model, which will you use along with various facilitative and analytic tools (The Craftsman role) to strengthen your performance in each of your other leadership functions?

With your roles accessible and your tools available, let's please return to where we began. Mobilizing is Job 1 for principals. You and your staff will identify or renew a shared focus on possible futures. You will declare your moonshot and freshly clarify the multiple paths you will take toward realizing the vital and essential ambitions you've defined ahead. As you commence, may I encourage you to pause regularly to accumulate and celebrate many small wins. ***Though not a distinct role we've emphasized, the effective principals I have known are also sincere and attentive cheerleaders. They regularly express deep and public appreciation for individual and collective effort. In those schools, acknowledgment builds collective persistence, courage, and a culture for continual progress.***

Nevertheless, though I have empowered you to envision, examine, and apply all that we have explored, **there has always been one vexing challenge inherent in any school or system in which I have worked. I believe it awaits your school's virtual daily attention and will demand thoughtfully crafted solutions.** Perhaps you are already grappling with it presently. I refer to this challenge as "the staggered start with common finishes" issue. In my view, no principal, school staff, or individual teacher can call and achieve a moonshot for all students to accomplish without meeting this often-universal challenge. Accordingly, and collaboratively, you and your school-community must fashion local theories of action to address it. After all, there is an implied promise we make to all our school's families; that wherever their children begin, they will grow into an enabled and possible future, even as they may be staggered behind others to finish their school journey.

Of Staggered Starts with Common Finishes

A Challenge for All Schools

In a track and field race of equal competitive length, runners who must begin the race from an assigned outside track lane position are given a forward and staggered start position significantly ahead of the runner on the inside lane whose start is coincident with the finish line. This staggering forward of starting positions for each successively outer lane along an 8-lane track compensates for and equalizes the race's distance for all contestants. Otherwise, each runner would have to run additional distance to the common finish line were everyone required to commence the race from the same starting line as the runner in the first interior lane.

Figuratively for a moment, let's imagine and consider a school year as a one-loop race around a 400-yard track. Not unlike a racetrack with its measured distance between the start and finish line, most school years are defined by an academic calendar of a fixed number of attendance days with a common start and end dates. Within that academic year's span of time, all students should learn a year of prescribed content and skills. Within this metaphor, each student is expected to complete one turn around the track of intended learning in not more than the academic calendar's fixed number of days.

However, school does not really function this way. It is not a direct 100-yard dash for all students down a straightaway track to an end of the year finish line. Actually, students vary in their readiness and capacities to complete the four 100-yard segments around our imagined 400-yard oval track. All school year "races" are not equivalent, though they are scheduled that way. If some of your students have accumulated learning deficits or continuing disabilities, they will have unique challenges to cross a common finish line (with its sets of performance indicators) by the specified end a particular school year. Their school year "race" around the track will begin in a reversely staggered rather than a forward-staggered order. Effectively, their learning race is more than 400 yards. It has to be completed at a faster or more efficient rate than the typical curriculum pacing calendar envisioned.

Nevertheless, as principal, **you must lead a school program for all of your students.** You must facilitate collaborative staff discourse to develop one or more immensely important theories of action. Together, you must determine how to apply your best understood professional knowledge and most impactful expertise to enable some of your students to have more than one year's growth and development in a fixed academic calendar year. Clearly, this will be more than just teaching faster. **It will require you closing students' varied learning gaps as symbolized in their many reversed and staggered starts of your school's "racetrack" each year.**

There is considerable research available to support your closing these gaps. Differentiation, curriculum compacting, diagnostic and accelerated learning resources, metacognitive goal setting, teacher-student conferencing, and literacy development are some worthy approaches to investigate and consider. So, too, are the student engagement practices highlighted in Chapter Three. Having posed the challenge, I urge you and your staff to bring local and affirmative solutions to life as you address this vexing dilemma on your shared watch.

Of Humility and Common Cause

As you consider where and how to begin, history provides you with critical lessons. Prepared leaders plan and do their best to understand current conditions and discern what is on the horizon. Wise leaders engage the best and brightest around them, study current data, and make projections to forecast future situations that may act as parameters for potential action. But history is also an often-cruel teacher. No leader and no team can be all-knowing. The truth is that in life and schools, tomorrow may bring forth the unanticipated. As a consequence, we do not always control the turning of our next page. Whether it is catastrophic weather, a pandemic virus, or a deranged invasive shooting, school leaders feel compelled to lead like a phoenix that must rise from among ashes. It would be best if you built the ark because the proverbial rain is torrential, and it is flooding. In these contexts, please know that you will learn, and you will lead even as you are humbled.

Some causes and commitments will always be so much more significant than each of us or our circumstances. The health of others, the welfare of family and friends, the sanctity of life, the value of listening and advanced preparation, the struggle to produce and connect to resources, the grace of reaching out to others, and the will to connect authentically with our students and families, these will be insights that shine brightly amid any unanticipated dark days filled with desperate trauma or disruptive chaos. These will be your fuel and your deliverance. And yet, knowing that the uncertainty is part of certainty, what is to be learned newly about time? Your time and that of those you lead will neither be infinite during upheaval or infinite in its opportunity to create anew.

My fellow educators and school leaders, under any conditions, our mission will always be critical. The promise we have to keep remains essential for every family. We elevate our students with capacities to join us in leading this world. Principals, even during disorienting days or the fog of the unforeseen, it will always be your time to lead with impact. With this volume, you have access to five leadership roles that can be your guides.

You will have your bully pulpit. What will you say? What are you saying now? Is there a new moonshot to declare, even though it will not be easy and maybe hard? As you survey and scan what's going on around you and the road ahead, you may need to confront new realities. Returning to school precisely as it was may not be an option. If not, how will you lead and engage others in creating new hybrid platforms and learning pathways? What will student-teacher and student-student engagement become? How will you collaborate, surface expertise, and share authority so that your faculty will commit to new quests and succeed? How may calendar tools support your developing a roadmap for your school's next 12-month cycle? What data do you have to understand your present circumstances, and what will you monitor to measure progress toward new goals? In the end, what will be your hypotheses and theories of action to move from your current state toward your newly considered desired future?

Colleagues, we are and shall remain in common cause. Be not afraid or deterred by a probable future filled with the currently unknowable or that will require you to address and potentially overcome the unexpected. Always begin using such challenging and disruptive times to reaffirm our shared purposes and plan freshly for what we do. *As a principal of impact, you will never close a book on your school as it was. Instead, you will stand ready to join with others to write new chapters even if the shared journey ahead is unclear.*

CLOSING THOUGHTS

Educating the next generation of young people to join with us in leading this world toward better ends is one of the most meaningful goals any person could elect as their life's work. Frankly, for me, this core purpose is one of the world's greatest and most important. Truly, I honor all educators who commit to and do this extraordinary work. Among them, effective school principals are particularly invaluable.

For you, my readers and future colleagues, I appreciate you joining me in this extended conversation about critical opportunities and imperatives for school leaders. Our students, our families, and our staff deserve nothing less from us.

Please permit me to leave you with these closing reflections. I have been blessed with many revelations and realizations during this lifetime spent within our shared profession. The most inspiring and humbling though are captured best in the renowned lines of Robert Frost's final stanza of his iconic poem, Stopping by Woods on a Snowy Evening. For me, they speak to educators of the implicit assurances we are pledged to undertake and the tireless commitment we must make to fulfilling them.

The woods are lovely, dark, and deep.
But I have promises to keep,
And miles to go before I sleep,
And miles to go before I sleep.

— Robert Frost, Vermont 1923[4]

---

4 Robert Frost, "Stopping by Woods on a Snowy Evening" from The Poetry of Robert Frost, edited by Edward Connery Lathem. Copyright 1923, © 1969 by Henry Holt and Company, Inc., renewed 1951, by Robert Frost. Reprinted with the permission of Henry Holt and Company, LLC.

APPENDIX

<u>Sample Facilitation Templates</u>

These sample templates serve as illustrative samples of collaborative facilitation tools and of a staff analysis and development framework. Among many disparate colleagues and clients, they have been originated, adapted, and used countless times in relation to a particular school, school system, or set of leadership needs. Always with collaborative consultation and advanced planning, they have helped school-communities to delineate present school conditions and beliefs, clarify school missions, and generate new visions. Ultimately, they have supported local determinations of what must be sustained, altered, or pursued newly to accomplish future goals and outcomes, as well as for whom.

- **Template A.1:**
  Mobilizing Questions and the Bully Pulpit

- **Template A.2:**
  Moonshot Thinking

- **Template A.3:**
  Shared Knowledge to Inform a Theory of Action

- **Template A.4:**
  Vision to Action

- **Template A.5:**
  Gaps to Goals

- **Template A.6:**
  Theory of Action

- **Template A.7:**
  A Staff Analysis Framework for Differentiation and Development

Inquiries or consultations regarding the creation, adaptation, and use of facilitation guides and the staff analysis framework are welcome. Contact information is available in the section entitled, *About the Author*.

Principals with Impact

PRINCIPALS WITH IMPACT
Appendix A
Template 1

MOBILIZING QUESTIONS
AND THE BULLY PULPIT

DIRECTIONS FOR USE: This purpose of this tool to engage school constituencies in a visioning and mobilization process. The notion of using one's "bully pulpit" was originated by President Theodore Roosevelt as a compelling opportunity to describe current realities and to espouse the needs and necessities to evolve toward bold possibilities and/or a new future. This inquiry guide poses four sets of questions that provide school participants with a guided forum for advocating and influencing professional points of view about current realities and to coalesce support for some perspectives while moving to act on others. Address each question of the four questions. Complete the table with relevant responses as they have arisen from the group's discussion.

1. WHERE ARE WE GOING?
Are we where we need to be in order to get to where we are going?

2. WHAT TELLS US WHERE WE ARE?
- *What progress have we made toward our intended goals, or not?*
- *What indicators tell us that this is so?*

3. ARE THERE CHANGES WE SHOULD CONSIDER?
- *Given where we are now, how might we evolve?*
- *Why is that reasonable and important for us to do at this time?*

4. ARE THERE GOALS WE HAVE NOT YET ATTEMPTED?
- *Are there places we need to be going now?*
- *Are there places we have never tried to get to?*
- *Is it urgent that we shift our target(s)? If so, how might we do so?*
- *What would be the evolved or newly identified goals?*

PROJECT TITLE: _____ SCHOOL/DEPARTMENT/GROUP: _____ DATE: _____

Principals with Impact

**PRINCIPALS
WITH IMPACT**
Appendix A
Template 2 – Page 1

MOONSHOT
THINKING

DIRECTIONS FOR PAGE ONE: In what became known as his 1962 Moon Speech, President Kennedy challenged our country to undertake what had previously been thought impossible, to land a man on the moon and return him safely to earth. Discuss President Kennedy's 1962 speech as represented in his excerpted questions found in column one. Each question has been adapted for a school setting. Address each question using the two table response columns. FOR PAGE TWO: Complete the four-part table with applicable responses to each question.

President Kennedy Quote	Responses	Discussion and Considerations
When considering the school's student results ... *"What is the goal (our Moonshot) which will serve to organize and measure the best of our energies and skills? ... the challenge we ... are willing to accept and no longer postpone?"* (e.g., a goal to be accomplished or a challenge to accept and not postpone?)	• • • • • • • •	
When considering the school's student results ... *"What is the challenge (our moonshot or professional goal) we are willing to win ... not because it is easy but because it is hard?"* (e.g., new student performance levels thought impossible to achieve?)	• • • • • • • •	

PROJECT TITLE: _____ SCHOOL/DEPARTMENT/GROUP: _____ DATE: _____

118

Principals with Impact

119

MOONSHOT
THINKING

PRINCIPALS WITH IMPACT
Appendix A
Template 2 – Page 2

CURRENT STATE

What is the school's Current State?

- ✓ What is working and what is not working?
- ✓ Based on what descriptors or body of evidence?
- ✓ What future external or internal factors may influence how your current state will evolve or change?

DESIRED FUTURE

What is the school's Desired Future?

- ✓ What is your Vision? Your "Moonshot?"
- ✓ Based on what descriptors or body of evidence?
- ✓ What future external or internal factors could influence how your current state may evolve or change?

WHO?

For who does your Current State analysis and Desired Future apply?

- ✓ Students?
- ✓ Families?
- ✓ Community?
- ✓ Staff?
- ✓ All of the above?

WHEN?

By when will you achieve your Desired Future? In what span of time?

PROJECT TITLE: _____   SCHOOL/DEPARTMENT/GROUP: _____   DATE: _____

155

Principals with Impact

PRINCIPALS WITH IMPACT
Appendix A
Template 3

SHARED KNOWLEDGE TO
INFORM A THEORY OF ACTION

A. What are the professional education, in-service training and/or research references and sources about high leverage and impactful teaching, learning, and assessment about which we already know?
B. From among these references and sources, which concepts or principles of practice will we choose for our collective theory of action to meet the needs of our students and therein, improve our students' results?

Professional Education, In-Service or Research -------- Concept or Principle of Practice	Professional Education, In-Service or Research -------- Concept or Principle of Practice	Professional Education, In-Service or Research -------- Concept or Principle of Practice
1. _____	2. _____	3. _____
Key Elements:	Key Elements:	Key Elements:
-	-	-
-	-	-
-	-	
-		
Reference(s) and Source(s) :	Reference(s) and Source(s):	Reference(s) and Source(s):

PROJECT TITLE: _____ SCHOOL/DEPARTMENT/GROUP: _____ DATE: _____

120

Principals with Impact

VISION TO ACTION

PRINCIPALS WITH IMPACT
Appendix A
Template 4

DIRECTIONS FOR USE: This template is a companion tool to the Gaps to Goals template. Use this first to review one or more important local mission, vision, goals and/or beliefs documents. Then using column one, select and excerpt specific key language you and colleagues may use to create inquiry questions to illuminate current practices and identify future potential areas for investigation or implementation. This is a precursor tool for developing hypotheses that may become your Theory of Action formulated with Template 6. Two example excerpts taken from a hypothetical school beliefs statement are provided as models for completing the template.

TWO EXAMPLE EXCERPTS	Possible Question(s) - Cluster 1	Possible Question(s) - Cluster 2	Possible Question(s) - Cluster 3
#1 - *"Continuous growth and improvement will occur for both students and staff when teachers identify, share and utilize best practices."*	What are the best practices to which our school is currently committed? Which are used consistently? Which are enabling us to get desired results? Considerations/Notes:	Are there best practices that have not been identified or incorporated into our work that will serve our needs or help to achieve our goals? Considerations/Notes:	What processes does our school use to examine and consider best practices? Are these adequate? Are these sufficient to address our future needs? Considerations/Notes:
#2 - *"Each student will engage in rigorous learning requiring developmentally appropriate higher order thinking."*	What does student engagement mean in our school? Does it vary? Are there patterns or trends? If so, are these engagement patterns consistent with our school goals for teaching and learning? Considerations/Notes:	What is rigorous learning? Is there research that defines what it is in practice? In our school, are common practices that promote rigorous learning consistently utilized in our classrooms? What is our evidence? Considerations/Notes:	What is our school's definition of higher order thinking? Are common taxonomies being utilized within lesson design? What developmentally appropriate practices are being used to support students' higher order thinking? Considerations/Notes:

Page 1

PROJECT TITLE: _____   SCHOOL/DEPARTMENT/GROUP: _____   DATE: _____

Principals with Impact

122

PRINCIPALS WITH IMPACT
Appendix A
Template 4

VISION TO ACTION

TEMPLATE

LOCAL EXCERPT	Possible Question(s) - Cluster 1	Possible Question(s) - Cluster 2	Possible Question(s) - Cluster 3
	Considerations/Notes:	Considerations/Notes:	Considerations/Notes:

LOCAL EXCERPT	Possible Question(s) - Cluster 1	Possible Question(s) - Cluster 2	Possible Question(s) - Cluster 3
	Considerations/Notes:	Considerations/Notes:	Considerations/Notes:

Page 2

PROJECT TITLE: _____   SCHOOL/DEPARTMENT/GROUP: _____   DATE: _____

Principals with Impact

PRINCIPALS WITH IMPACT
Appendix A
Template 5

FROM GAPS TO GOALS

DIRECTIONS FOR USE: This template is a tool that builds upon and follows from use of the Vision to Action template. Staff will have developed and responded to self-generated inquiry questions used to consider currently valued beliefs and practices. Additionally, they will have identified gaps that may exist between actual current practice and desired or projected future practices. Use this companion template to identify actions to address the gaps. To do so, you will identify a focus area for future actions, describe the gap(s) identified, and state the goal to be achieved once the gap is filled or addressed. Three columns with guiding questions are provided for developing actions steps.

FOCUS AREA:

GAP IDENTIFIED:

GOAL IDENTIFIED:

SCHOOL/GRADE/DEPT:

WHAT DO WE NEED TO **PLAN or ORGANIZE?**	WHAT DO WE NEED TO **LEARN?**	WHAT DO WE NEED TO **DEVELOP and/or IMPLEMENT?**

PROJECT TITLE: _____   SCHOOL/DEPARTMENT/GROUP: _____   DATE: _____

THEORY OF ACTION

PRINCIPALS WITH IMPACT
Appendix A
Template 6

DIRECTIONS FOR USE: Write specific SCHOOL- BASED (or DEPT-BASED) GOALS with a related Theory of Action for each of three priority areas that if incorporated into an overall action plan and implemented will achieve measurable results during the _____ year.

GOAL AREA #1	Describe Action(s) you will take	Based on a research rationale or data based theory for why this will work.	Explain or identify what your metrics or deliverables will be
Insert a Unique Title for this Goal Area	If we _____ *Complete Sentence Stem* *Insert a Brief Explanation*	Then _____ will happen *Complete Sentence Stem*	And we will see this result in _____ as measured or indicated by _____. *Complete Sentence Stem*

Page 1

PROJECT TITLE: _____ SCHOOL/DEPARTMENT/GROUP: _____ DATE: _____

124

160

Principals with Impact

THEORY OF ACTION

PRINCIPALS WITH IMPACT
Appendix A
Template 6

GOAL AREA #2	*Describe Action(s) you will take*	*Based on a research rationale or data based theory for why this will work.*	*Explain or identify what your metrics or deliverables will be*
	If we _____	Then _____ will happen	And we will see this result in _____ as measured or indicated by _____
Insert a Unique Title for this Goal Area	*Complete Sentence Stem*	*Complete Sentence Stem*	*Complete Sentence Stem*
	Insert a Brief Explanation		

GOAL AREA #3	*Describe Action(s) you will take*	*Based on a research rationale or data based theory for why this will work.*	*Explain or identify what your metrics or deliverables will be*
	If we _____	Then _____ will happen	And we will see this result in _____ as measured or indicated by _____
Insert a Unique Title for this Goal Area	*Complete Sentence Stem Here*	*Complete Sentence Stem Here*	*Complete Sentence Stem Here*
	Insert a Brief Explanation:		

TEMPLATE

125

Page 2

PROJECT TITLE: _____   SCHOOL/DEPARTMENT/GROUP: _____   DATE: _____

126

STAFF ANALYSIS TOOL

PRINCIPALS WITH IMPACT
Appendix A
Template 7

This **STAFF ANALYSIS FRAMEWORK** is a recording and classification tool. When completed, it creates and depicts a holistic scatterplot of your entire staff. It begins by identifying your analysis of each staff member's relative position within the four-quadrant matrix. The variables of analysis are correlated with the two axes and the Key.

The analysis lens for each staff member's plot point is referenced against a school's **THEORY OF ACTION** to achieve specific student results. This is represented in the question:

"What actions if taken or principles of practice if used with consistency, will achieve our desired results?"

The X-axis assesses each staff member's actions as measured by his or her frequency in implementing those specific lesson design constructs or principles of pedagogy to which the school has committed for elevating student results. **The Y-axis assesses** each staff member's levels of knowledge and skill for effectively applying those same constructs or strategies. **The related plot point (XY)** will place each staff member in one of four quadrants.

After plotting each staff member's data point on this same quadrant grid, a school-wide distribution pattern will be depicted regarding the Theory of Action element(s) being implemented frequently and effectively.

Theory of Action Exercise

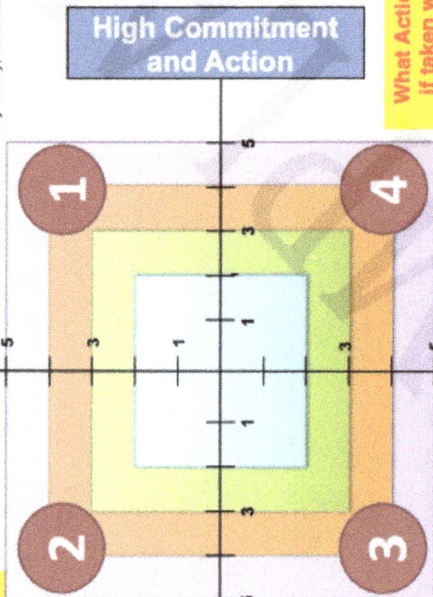

High Commitment and Action

Highly Knowledgeable, Skilful and Effective

Limited Knowledge, Skill or Efficacy

Limited Commitment or Action

What Actions, if taken with consistency, will achieve our desired results?

KEY
5 = Most of the Time (> 90%)
4 = (75 – 89% of the time)
3 = At Least Half the Time (50 – 74%)
2 = (25 – 49% of the ime)
1 = Very Rarely; but at Least Once

1   4

2   3

5   3   1   1   3   5

A FOUR-QUADRANT MATRIX AN EXAMPLE OF USING THE KEY AND AXES SCALES
A "5X5" Quadrant 1 teacher would be one who demonstrates the highest levels of knowledge, skill and effectiveness in implementing your school's THEORY OF ACTION principals of practice " most of the time" (i.e., with greater than 90% frequency on both ends of the "High" or "Highly" labeled axes.)

PROJECT TITLE: _____   SCHOOL/DEPARTMENT/GROUP: _____   DATE: _____

List of Role Referenced Diagrams

ABOUT THE AUTHOR

Dr. Jaeger's experience is wide-ranging across a diverse range of PK-12 public school systems. They have been small and midsize, suburban and urban, multicultural and more homogeneous, and either centralized as systems or regionally organized as county consortiums.

During his four-decade career, he has served as a schoolteacher and university professor, school assistant principal, and principal, deputy superintendent for curriculum and instruction, school district superintendent of schools, and as an appointed state education department member for its professional standards and practices advisory council. His many local and national workshops have focused on strategic planning, data-driven school improvement, teacher and principal evaluation, new teacher induction, instructional design, technology integration and blended learning, coaching for improved practice, arts-in-education integration, interdisciplinary instruction, and curriculum development.

Dr. Jaeger earned a B.A. from Amherst College and an M.A., M.Ed., and Ed.D. from Teachers College, Columbia University. He has been recognized for Excellence in Administration, and distinguished service to youth meriting with both a National Parent Teacher Association Honorary Lifetime Membership and the Literacy Volunteers of America L.I.F.E. Award.

Dr. Jaeger is President of Learning and Leadership Services, LLC. His continuing consultant work is customized collaboratively to support school leaders, faculties, district leadership teams, community organizations, public charter schools, and boards of education.

For further information or inquiries regarding in-person or video-based consultant services, contact Dr. Jaeger at learningleadershipservices.com.

LEARNING &
LEADERSHIP
S E R V I C E S

www.ingramcontent.com/pod-product-compliance
Lightning Source LLC
Chambersburg PA
CBHW052342210326
41597CB00037B/6225